What to do about

Equal Pay
for Women

What to do about

Equal Pay for Women

G. L. BUCKINGHAM

Gower Press

First published in Great Britain by Gower Press Limited, Epping, Essex, 1973

ISBN 0 7161 0213 7

Set in 11pt Imprint and printed in Great Britain by
Robert MacLehose and Company Limited
The University Press, Glasgow.

Contents

Tables

Foreword

This book is designed to provide a plain man's guide to the Equal Pay Act. Its justification, if any is needed, is that, half way through the period of time which the Act allows before it comes into force, many companies do not appear to have examined the effect that the Act will have upon their pay and industrial relations situation.

I have written this book on the basis of personal experience of the effect that the Act will have in an industry and company in which large numbers of women are employed. Industries and companies which employ a substantial proportion of women cannot afford to ignore the effect that the Equal Pay Act will have upon them. Yet in 1973 it is apparent that many managements have still not reached conclusions and have not developed plans to comply with the requirements of the Act when it comes into force on 29 December 1975.

The book is based on a positive approach to the requirements of the Equal Pay Act and reflects the spirit on which the Act is based. Thus the reader who hopes to find that this book will provide the means to avoid implementing the Act in a comprehensive and equitable manner will be disappointed. Unlike a famous article which appeared some two years ago in a widely read management journal, this book does not provide a checklist of methods by which management may avoid the obligations that the Equal Pay Act places on them. Rather, it urges them to take a planned and positive approach to the implications of equal pay, and where trade unions are concerned to involve full-time officials and employee representatives in analysing the problems arising from equal pay and in proposing means whereby the requirements of the Act can be met.

After 1975 some companies will suddenly find they are required to answer before an industrial tribunal a claim by a female employee that they are not meeting the requirements of the Equal Pay Act. By the end of 1975, reference to industrial tribunals will be a widely known and established feature of British industrial relations. Thus we must expect many women to be willing to take their case to industrial tribunals and if they succeed the effect upon the payment and industrial relations situation in the company concerned could be serious.

The Act is full of ambiguities. These will only be interpreted by the industrial tribunals and the National Industrial Relations Court and, as case law develops, many companies may find that they are in an exposed situation. But if they take the advice contained in this book and analyse the effect that the provisions of the Act will have, make their plans accordingly and negotiate and consult about the implementation of these plans with employees and their trade unions, their position should be secure.

The book limits itself to the actual effect of the Equal Pay Act. There is no doubt however that this Act should be seen as a forerunner to the more fundamental question of equal opportunity and the extent to which industry and commerce should open its job and career opportunities to women. Equal opportunity is a more far reaching and emotional subject.

As a male chauvinist, I am obviously entering into a controversial area if I dare to give a view on this subject. Nevertheless, I would suggest that the whole issue of equal opportunity is clouded with emotion and that there are a number of paradoxes in the debate which is currently taking place about this subject at national level. On the one hand women are claiming, with some justification, that their opportunities in industry and commerce are limited by male prejudice. On the other hand, academics, trade unions and some management are increasingly bringing to society's attention the motivational and industrial relations problems caused by the organization of work in industry and commerce. On the one hand employees are increasingly concerned about the boring and repetitious nature of much of the work that they are asked to undertake and these problems are a subject of increasing concern at industry, national and governmental level. On the other hand, women are claiming that they are being excluded from opportunities in industry and commerce even though what they appear to be demanding has manifestly failed to satisfy many of their male counterparts. Any resolution of these problems depends upon a radical rethinking about the nature of industrial society today. It is beyond the scope of this book to deal with such a problem but it is a perspective which may be useful for practising managers to retain at the back of their minds when considering the implications of the Equal Pay Act.

Acknowledgements

Many people have contributed to the production of this book. I should like to thank Mr Peter Graham-Woollard for checking the proofs and for making many valuable suggestions; Mr J. J. Scullion and Miss P. Malpass for providing much of the statistical information contained in the book, and in particular, Miss Kay Kendall for bearing the whole load of typing the book, draft after draft, with her customary speed and accuracy. Hers was a major contribution to the production of this book and my sincere thanks are due to her, and my other colleagues who have given me so much help.

Finally, I must thank my wife and children for their forbearance during this period when they saw little of me; the phrase 'publish and be damned' took on a new connotation at this time!

I

How the Equal Pay Act came about

The Royal Assent to the Equal Pay Act, given in the last hours of the Labour government in 1970, marked a turning point for women in employment in Great Britain, for their employers and for the trade unions which represent women in increasing numbers. It marked the end of this country's widespread use of its actual or potential female workforce as a 'cheap resource'. The Act gave each employed woman the legislative right, from 29 December 1975, to receive the same pay as her male colleagues if her job is the same or similar. It further gave women the right to equal treatment to male colleagues where job-evaluation schemes are or will be in operation. It presaged a fundamental reappraisal by society of the employment of women in Britain and implied a renewed interest in and consideration of the more fundamental question of women's opportunity (or lack of it) in employment. This question has already come to the fore and has recently been considered by a select committee of the House of Lords, and been the subject of a private members' Bill in the House of Commons. Legislation to establish women's rights to equal opportunity must be a strong possibility in the next few years.

In the shorter term, however, the Equal Pay Act may reduce

women's employment opportunities. Employers have been slow to work out the implications the Equal Pay Act has for them, but three years after it became law it is becoming apparent that the additional costs of employing women are reducing job opportunities in an economy which, until 1973, has obstinately refused to grow faster than a beggarly 1–2 per cent per annum.

The trade union movement, while critical of some aspects of the Act, saw it nevertheless as a major success, even though some individual unions regarded it with indifference or even downright hostility. The TUC could claim with some justification that it had been the principal group pressuring the government to pass the Act. But this pressure represented a major shift of opinion in the trade union movement. At TUC conferences since the turn of the century lip service had been paid to the principle of equal pay: impressive resolutions were passed by overwhelming votes, after which the conferences could move on to more weighty subjects with a clear conscience. Why had no progress been made and so little pressure applied by the trade union movement during this period? The TUC's explanation is that it was because the intention of trade unions, the majority of which included few women, had primarily been to protect the job prospects of the men.[1] To be brutal, it may be that this relative indifference can be more simply ascribed to the almost total male domination of the British trade unions and their essentially conservative and pragmatic nature. As the most representative institutions of the working class, the trade unions inevitably reflected the working man's beliefs and values.

> The point of departure for an understanding of the position of the working class father in his home is that he is the boss there, 'the master in his own house' . . . there is likely to be a deference to him as the main breadwinner . . . He remains the chief contact with the outer world which puts the money into the house.[2]

However, the old order changed and as in so many spheres the Second World War shook the established order and tradition.

Women's contribution to the war effort was widespread and vital in the factories in particular. As a result, at the height of the war in 1944 the British government set up a Royal Commission to consider 'the social, economic and financial implications of the claim of equal pay for equal work'. The Commission's report was cautious on the principle of equal pay and comprehensive in detailing the reasons why women could not expect equal treatment. However, this report was not without influence on successive governments in the post-war period. From about 1955 female staff employed in the Civil Service, local government and in the nationalized industries moved over a seven-year period to full equal pay. However, this important equal pay programme in the public sector only applied to those jobs undertaken by both men and women. Jobs which were exclusively done by women (typists for example) were not covered by this equal pay programme. Furthermore, this programme did not extend to manual workers in the public sector nor did it have any marked influence on private industry, and commerce, which tended to ignore the significance of this important development.

EQUAL PAY IN THE EEC

The trend however was clear for all to see and the pressures for equal pay were not limited to Great Britain, rather the reverse. In 1951 the International Labour Organization had adopted the principle of equal pay in its Convention 100, while article 119 of the Treaty of Rome (which established the European Economic Community) laid down that each member country shall 'maintain the application of the principle that men and women should receive equal pay for equal work'. By 1969 all the Common Market countries were ahead of the United Kingdom in progress towards equal pay even though such progress had been slower than the Commission had hoped. The Commission estimated optimistically that between 80 and 85 per cent of women working in the six member countries of the EEC were paid the rate for the job on an equal basis with men. The facts suggested otherwise however. For example, even in France where the greatest progress had been made the differential between the earnings of men and women by the late 1960s was over 7 per cent. In Germany considerable discrimination in earnings existed, often by means of an artificial distinction between 'heavy' and 'light' work. Heavy work became a means of defining work done by men and also a means of justifying a pay differential for the male worker.

The Common Market countries had, nevertheless, made much more progress towards equal pay than Britain by the end of the decade and this fact contributed to the pressures for legislation. Other influential voices, besides the TUC, made themselves heard on this subject. For example, the Institute of Personnel Management which, in 1963, had given general support to the principle of equal pay, came out early in 1969 with a comprehensive policy statement on equal pay for the consideration of the then Department of Employment and Productivity. The Institute accepted 'the principle that Britain should advance towards the practice of equal pay for work of equal value'. It stressed the need for enough time to allow a phased introduction of equal pay and proposed that 'the phasing must be flexible enough to enable industries and organizations with special problems to move at a different pace'. It suggested that a limited number of pilot exercises to introduce equal pay should be considered in a few selected companies before the government embarked on new legislation, arguing that such experiments 'would not only speed up the introduction of equal pay but would provide valuable information on which to base future legislation'.

NEED FOR LEGISLATION

However, by the time this report was published, the Labour government had come to the conclusion that legislation was needed to establish women's rights to equal pay. Strong opposition to the introduction of equal pay existed, while many companies which accepted the principle were unwilling to introduce equal pay if their competitors refused to do so. These arguments were particularly relevant in labour-intensive industries which employed large numbers of women, such as textiles, footwear and retailing.

In 1968 a tripartite working party was set up representing the government, the Confederation of British Industry and the Trades Union Congress to investigate the effect equal pay for equal work would have on the country's wage and salary bill. As the possibility of legislation grew stronger so opponents to the concept of equal pay became more vociferous. Among the reasons put forward at this time to justify inequality of pay were:

1 That men are stronger and more efficient than women.
2 That men are prepared to invest more in themselves by such means as job training and apprenticeships than are women.
3 That in western society men are much more firmly the principal source of manpower as it is the role of the male to be the principal provider to the family unit.
4 That women place more importance on the non-monetary aspects of their job than do men.
5 That if paid equally women would be more costly than men as they are less reliable in their attendance and their labour turnover is higher.

Such arguments were strongly rebutted by the proponents of equal pay who claimed that unequal pay was a particularly clear example of the discrimination against women in society by employers, workers' organizations and society at large, all of whom are completely male dominated. Equal pay became a major focal point for the growing women's liberation movement which crossed the Atlantic at about this time and which found a notable, not to say notorious, champion in an Australian lecturer at Warwick University, Germaine Greer.

Miss Greer in her book *The Female Eunuch*[3] presented a passionate case for society to release the true potential of women and struck at male dominance, advocating the emergence of the revolutionary woman for whom 'the struggle which is not joyous is the wrong struggle'.[4] The book was published a few months after the 1969 TUC conference which 'rang with stirring speeches by female delegates and pledged itself to prosecuting the struggle for equal pay for equal work'.[5] However, Miss Greer unkindly mentions that while Congress rang to such pledges, nobody mentioned that female clerks at TUC headquarters Congress House were earning less than their male colleagues. She also pointed out that at this conference there were only 51 women delegates and more than 1200 men.

Nevertheless, Miss Greer did less than justice to the 1969 TUC conference. The stage had been set by the women machinists in the Ford plant at Dagenham who earlier in the year had struck for equal pay under the recently established job-evaluation system, which Ford had introduced, covering all manual workers. At the Congress it was the Transport and General Workers Union and its then general secretary, Frank Cousins, which gave Congress an unequivocal lead.

The Transport and General Workers Union used one of the two resolutions which it was entitled to put before Congress to demand equal pay for work of equal value. The resolution was carried overwhelmingly and this time there was a Labour government in power, and the Secretary of State for Employment and Productivity was a woman—Mrs Barbara Castle. Within a year, the Equal Pay Act was on the statute book.

REFERENCES

1 E. Chipchase, Secretary, Women's Advisory Committee, TUC in report to International Pay Conference, October 1972.
2 Richard Hoggart, *Uses of Literacy,* Penguin, 1958, p.54.
3 Germaine Greer, *The Female Eunuch,* MacGibbon & Kee, 1970.
4 Ibid, p. 20.
5 Ibid, p. 117.

2

What the Act provides

In October 1969 the Labour government circulated a consultative document to interested parties setting out its considered ideas for an Equal Pay Act. The climate of opinion in the country had developed by this time to the extent that not only were the three principal political parties and the TUC in favour of legislation to establish the right of women to equal pay, but so was the Confederation of British Industry. However, although there was widespread agreement to the principle of legislation on equal pay, there was less unanimity on the form, content and timing of any Act. Thus the government's consultative document sought to lay down the principles on which the Act would be based and raised a number of important issues on which those most affected by the Act were asked to give their views.

THE TIMETABLE

On one major issue, however, the government had already made up its mind, namely the date by which the Act would be implemented. In announcing its intention to introduce legislation on equal pay, the government had unequivocally stated that such an Act would provide for the full implementation of equal pay by

31 December 1975. This date was a disappointment to the TUC
which wanted a shorter timescale and which continued to press for
1972 as the target date.

The CBI had naturally looked for as long a period of implementation as possible. With this in mind the employers had proposed
1977 or 1978 as a realistic objective and, although the government
had not accepted this proposal, the CBI were satisfied with the date
announced. Employers would have six years over which to plan
the introduction of equal pay and to implement the necessary
decisions on manpower and investment so as to absorb, wherever
possible, the increased costs involved.

So the date for full implementation remained the end of 1975.
However, to meet some of the TUC's objections to the length of
this implementation period, an additional timetable provision was
included in the Act. Under section 9(2) the Secretary of State was
given the power to secure orderly progress towards equal pay by
laying an order before Parliament requiring partial implementation
of the Act by 31 December 1973. In particular such an order,
under section 9(3), would provide 'in respect of rates of pay, that
the rate to be paid to a person . . . shall not be less than nine-tenths
of the rate paid to those with whom comparison is required . . . '.
In other words, the Secretary of State could require women's
rates of pay to be raised to at least 90 per cent of men's rates by
the end of 1973.

In the event the Conservative government did not take these
powers but gave its own impetus to the orderly progress to equal
pay under Stage Two of its Counter-Inflation Policy. This will be
considered in Chapter 3.

THE OVERALL PLAN

The general plan of the Act is on the following lines. The fundamental requirement is that there should be no discrimination in
remuneration on grounds of sex. If such discrimination is alleged
to exist, an aggrieved party—for example a woman in employment
or a trade union representing her—can take the case to an indus-

trial tribunal which is empowered to make an award under the terms of the Act. It is possible to appeal against an industrial tribunal's interpretation of the law (but not against its interpretation of the facts of a case) to the National Industrial Relations Court.

The decision to use industrial tribunals as the legal institutions basically responsible for ensuring compliance with the Act is important. It represents a further extension of the scope of these tribunals which were set up under the Industrial Training Act of 1964 and given more work by the Redundancy Payments Act of 1965. The tribunals were designed to provide a prompt and relatively informal network of labour courts to which individual employees could easily refer. They were established on a nationwide basis and their administrative and procedural requirements were deliberately kept as simple and unencumbered as possible. The reason for giving the tribunals powers under the Equal Pay Act was that women, or their representative organizations, would be assured of easy access to a legal body should they consider themselves to be denied fair treatment under the Act. This policy was reinforced by the decision in 1972 that appeals against industrial tribunal rulings should be heard by the National Industrial Relations Court which also has simple and informal rules of procedure. Accordingly, it is to be hoped, long drawn out legal delays are unlikely to occur between parties in dispute over any aspect of the Act. This will be of real benefit to the individual employee and the implications will have to be carefully considered by every employer. For the latter a policy of procrastination or evasion, under the guise of legal technicalities, will not be one of the options available.

COLLECTIVE AGREEMENTS AND COMPANY WAGE STRUCTURES

The Act recognizes that nearly all women employees are paid according to a wage structure that is applied throughout a company or throughout an industry. In some cases the structure is decided by management alone; often it is the result of collective bargaining with unions; for a large number of women workers it is established by a wages council. It is, therefore, of crucial importance to deal with company-wide and industry-wide wage structures in order to achieve equal treatment for women.

Section 3 of the Act covers collective agreements and company wage structures. The section makes it clear that these are to be regarded as discriminatory under the Act if they contain any provision applying specifically to men only or to women only. This covers, of course, provisions that specify separate rates of pay for men and women doing the same job; it also means that provisions that specify a 'women's rate' irrespective of type of work will be considered discriminatory.

Section 3 gives any party to an agreement the right to apply to the Industrial Arbitration Board to have discriminatory provisions removed from the agreement. The Secretary of State may apply to the Board to have a company wage structure altered if it is discriminatory.

Sections 4 and 5 make similar provisions with respect to wages regulation orders and agricultural wages orders.

This provision is of fundamental importance and it is possible that its significance was not fully recognized at the time the Act was passing through Parliament. The great majority of women in employment are affected and will benefit from the Act because it prohibits collective agreements from discriminating on a sex basis. Much of the discussion during the passage of the Act centred on arguments about the definitions of equal or similar work and what the phrase 'equal value' meant. Far less attention was paid to this important section of the Act and its far reaching effect has only become apparent since.

The effect of this section of the legislation can be best illustrated by the following examples:

Example A

Many collective agreements negotiated at national level include a number of rates for men, depending on the category of work which they undertake, but only have one 'women's rate'. This serves as the basic minimum for all categories of work undertaken by women in the industry. The engineering industry is perhaps the best known example of this type of agreement with male rates established for both skilled and unskilled male categories but only one rate for women. Under the Equal Pay Act this distinction will not be permitted after the end of 1975. Skilled women in the engineering industry will receive the skilled rate, and other women covered by the agreement, the unskilled male rate as their basic minimum.

Example B
In other industries male rates of pay are negotiated covering the skilled, semi-skilled and unskilled categories of work. In such cases, separate women's rates for these categories of work will disappear after 1975 and the male rates for the appropriate category will be applied to the women concerned.

The far reaching implications of this part of the Act on differentials in plants across a company is considered in Chapter 7.

'Like work'
The first section of the Equal Pay Act states that:

> The provisions of this section shall have effect with a view to securing that employers give equal treatment as regards terms and conditions of employment to men and to women, that is to say that (subject to the provisions of this section and of section 6 below)—
>
> (*a*) For men and women employed on like work the terms and conditions of one sex are not in any respect less favourable than those of the other.

In section 1 (4) the Act gives a comprehensive definition of the phrase 'like work':

> A woman is to be regarded as employed on like work with men, if, but only if, her work and theirs is of the same or a broadly similar nature, and the differences (if any) between the things she does and the things they do are not of practical importance in relation to terms and conditions of employment;

and accordingly in comparing her work with theirs regard shall be had to the frequency or otherwise with which any such differences occur in practice as well as to the nature and extent of the differences.

This section appears likely to be a lawyer's paradise. The sentence 'the things they do are not of practical importance in relation to terms and conditions of employment' is capable of a multitude of interpretations. It is important to note the emphasis on the words 'do' and 'does'. If a woman does not 'do' shift work or 'does' not work certain hours required by the male jobs she cannot claim equal pay under this section. If she 'does' not undertake the range of duties in a male job or 'does' not undergo a similar training period then her claim may not be upheld. Such differences would be, one might think, of considerable practical importance in comparing two jobs.

The remaining part of this section is similarly ambiguous. It clearly suggests that jobs may be 'like' if any differences between them, even if they are large ones, occur only occasionally, and that a number of differences may be ignored if they are only small ones. Here again we are in the realm of value judgements which will remain unclear until the references to the industrial tribunals establish case law. The consultative document recognised that this was likely to be the case in stating. 'It would in the last resort be for the tribunal to decide whether the differences were, in fact, slight in any particular case'. In the meantime, managers can only examine on a common sense basis the content, skills and responsibilities of male and female jobs in the same plant or office and decide the degree of 'likeness', if any.

This section of the Act already goes further than the narrowest interpretation of equal pay, namely that pay should only be the same where jobs are absolutely identical. Section 1(5) takes the scope of the Act very much further.

'Equal Value'

The 1970 Equal Pay Act gives legislative recognition in clear and unambiguous terms to the technique of job evaluation. It states that:

A woman is to be regarded as employed on work rated as equivalent with that of any men if, but only if, her job and their job have been given an equal value, in terms of the demand made on a worker under various headings (for instance effort, skill, decision) on a study undertaken with a view to evaluating in those terms the jobs to be done by all or any of the employees in an undertaking or group of undertakings, or would have been given an equal value but for the evaluation being made on a system setting different values for men and women on the same demand under any heading.

This is a comprehensive definition of the most common form of job evaluation—the 'factor plan' system. The Act with a surprising degree of sophistication recognizes that existing schemes may differentiate between men and women in their technical construction and forbids it in the future.

As will be discussed more fully in Chapter 5 job evaluation schemes have been applied to an increasing extent in recent years. Many of the largest companies in the private sector have introduced job evaluation for both manual workers and clerical employees where the majority of women are employed. As a result, such companies are clearly covered by this provision of the Act, but furthermore must check carefully to ensure that there is no discrimination in the design of their existing job evaluation schemes. As the consultative document explained: 'This proposal would not mean that all women's work had to be evaluated. The question of possible discrimination in this sense would arise only if and when a job evaluation exercise was carried out . . .'.

TERMS AND CONDITIONS OF EMPLOYMENT

The Act is not limited to establishing equal pay between men and women. Section 1(1) states that its aim is to ensure that, with certain specified exceptions, 'employers give equal treatment as regards terms and conditions of employment to men and to women . . .'. Thus, its scope extends to a wide range of employment conditions, for example, hours of work, holiday entitlements, shifts and overtime premiums, service pay, periods of notice and so on. Most companies do not differentiate in conditions of employment between their male and female employees but some examples of differences may well exist.

The consultative document highlighted one major difference in conditions of employment which the Act would affect, namely, the age at which the full adult rate of pay is paid.

The document pointed out that many women received the adult rate at 18 while men generally waited until 21 for the full rate. However, under the proposed legislation 'men's and women's rates between the ages of 18 and 21 would have to be equalized. Either the women would have to be put on men's rates or the men on the women's rates or there would have to be a mixture of both procedures'. The consultative document sought views on whether or not the legislation should make specific provisions to equalize the age at which adult rates are paid. In the event, the Equal Pay Act did not make explicit provisions to cover this point, but the need to establish equal treatment in this aspect of conditions of employment is clearly implied under section 1(1).

However, certain conditions of employment do not have to be made the same for men and women. These are defined in section 6. First, where women's terms and conditions of employment are 'in any respect, affected by compliance with the law regulating the employment of women' (for example and notably part 6 of the Factories Act 1961) then the provisions of the Equal Pay Act do not apply. The safeguard for women under the Factories Act remain therefore and the limitations on shift work, night work and periods of work without a break for women remain and do not apply to men.

Second, and not surprisingly, the Act does not seek to remove 'any special treatment . . . accorded to women in connection with the birth or expected birth of a child'. Maternity allowances, periods of leave without pay for expectant mothers and similar special arrangements can continue and the mere male cannot claim equal treatment in respect of such uniquely female benefits where they exist.

Finally, and most important, the Act does not seek to cover any aspect of retirement 'whether voluntary or not, on grounds of age, length of service or incapacity'. Thus the Act does not require an equal retirement age for men and women or equal pension entitlements and indeed the Conservative government's social security legislation perpetuates the retirement age of 60 for women and 65 for men and thus maintains this anomalous distinction. Employers do not have to provide the same pension arrangements or entitlements to men and women under the Equal Pay Act or the same redundancy provisions where these relate to an early pension or the same ill-health retirement benefits if these are based on a pension. Ill-health or redundancy provisions will have to be identical however if they are structured on any pay-related basis.

CONCLUSION

All parties gave the Act general support during its passage through Parliament although the Conservatives tended to stress the practical difficulties which would be encountered in applying the Act. Mrs Barbara Castle, who piloted the Bill through the House, emphasized that it was a first important step to removing discrimination against women and during the third reading told her women supporters that she was 'providing a statutory framework, not spoon-feeding'. She pointed out that of 8.5 million women in employment at that time only 1 million received equal pay. It was her hope that the Act would cover a further 6 million women by 1975. This gave some indication of the size of the problem and the costs involved for many companies.

3

Pay differentials
as they are today

Between 1946 and 1971 the number of women in the working population increased by over 100 per cent from nearly 4 million to over 8 million. In 1946 one third of the working population were women and by 1971 this proportion had risen to over 38 per cent.

The proportions of women in different industries vary greatly. Only 30 per cent of women in employment work in manufacturing companies compared with 43 per cent of males who are in employment.

As Table 3:1 shows, much larger proportions of women are to be found in the retail and distributive trades.

Table 3:1 identifies the industries which will experience the greatest effect of the Equal Pay Act, notably clothing and footwear, textiles, food, drink and tobacco, together with the insurance and banking industries.

When the numbers of women according to occupation are examined, the majority is to be found in unskilled and semi-skilled work in both the manual and non-manual categories. The most notable trend in recent years has been the steady increase in

Table 3:1   Employees in employment (June 1971)

Industry group	Number		Females as percentage of	
	Males	*Females*	all employees in each industry group	all females in all industries and services
	thousands	*thousands*	%	%
Total, all industries and services	13 542	8 486	38.5	100.0
Total, all manufacturing industries	5 855	2 576	30.6	30.4
Agriculture, forestry, fishing	278	66	19.2	0.8
Mining and quarrying	384	18	4.4	0.2
Food, drink and tobacco	489	348	41.6	4.1
Coal and petroleum products	50	8	13.0	0.1
Chemicals and allied industries	332	134	28.7	1.6
Metal manufacture	486	69	12.4	0.8
Mechanical engineering	952	191	16.7	2.2
Instrument engineering	101	57	36.1	0.7
Electrical engineering	541	340	38.6	4.0
Shipbuilding and marine engineering	177	14	7.5	0.2
Vehicles	708	105	12.9	1.2
Metal goods not elsewhere specified	428	187	30.4	2.2
Textiles	326	286	46.7	3.4
Leather, leather goods and fur	30	22	41.8	0.3
Clothing and footwear	122	350	74.1	4.1
Bricks, pottery, glass, cement	253	72	22.2	0.8
Timber, furniture, etc.	236	57	19.4	0.7
Paper, printing, publishing	411	207	33.4	2.4
Other manufacturing industries	213	131	38.1	1.5

Table 3:1   *continued*

Industry group	Number		Females as percentage of	
	Males	*Females*	*all employees in each industry group*	*all females in all industries and services*
	thousands	*thousands*	*%*	*%*
Construction	1 163	85	6.8	1.0
Gas, electricity and water	306	63	17.1	0.7
Transport and communication	1 280	284	18.1	3.3
Distributive trades	1 127	1 455	56.3	17.1
Insurance, banking, finance and business services	458	513	52.8	6.0
Miscellaneous services	800	993	55.4	11.7
Professional and scientific services	943	1 961	67.5	23.1
Public administration and defence	945	471	33.3	5.6

Source: the first Office of Manpower Economics Report on the implementation of the Equal Pay Act 1970, HMSO, 1972

the number of women in clerical jobs. Over two thirds of the clerical jobs in the country are now occupied by women as are well over half the shop assistant jobs in the retail trade. While the proportion of women in the clerical and distributive areas has risen then over the last two decades there appears to have been a reduction in the percentage employed in professional, supervisory and technical jobs. Table 3:2 compares male and female numbers and percentage of the total of each sex employed in manufacturing industry in May 1968.

Table 3:2 clearly indicates that the effect of the Equal Pay Act on manufacturing industry is to be felt among two categories of employee—semi-skilled production workers and clerical employees. In both of these areas there are substantial numbers of male and female workers. Many of the production workers are covered by

B

collective agreements negotiated on an industry-wide national basis, while as will be shown in a later chapter, job evaluation is increasingly applied to clerical employees in the larger companies at least.

Table 3:2 Proportions of male and female employees in manufacturing industry in May 1968

	Males		Females	
	Number	Percentage of men	Number	Percentage of women
Managers and superintendents	397 350	9.3	18 060	1.0
Scientists and technologists	92 150	2.2	2 855	0.2
Draughtsmen	104 690	2.5	1 455	0.1
Other technicians	183 240	4.3	13 750	0.7
Clerical/office staff	345 220	8.1	572 670	31.7
Other technical and administrative staff	274 860	6.4	56 420	3.1
Skilled craft and production workers	1 547 480	36.2	70 495	3.9
Semi-skilled production workers	1 326 440	31.0	1 071 940	59.3

Source: Department of Employment

It should be noted that the proportion of women in employment in the UK is very similar to other western European countries. Thus there are 53 women at work for every 100 male workers in the UK and this compares closely with 56 women per 100 male workers in West Germany, 52 women per 100 male workers in the USA and 50 women per 100 male workers in France. This proportion is radically different in the USSR where the women in employment slightly outnumber the men (102 women to 100 men).

THE PAY RELATIONSHIPS OF MEN AND WOMEN

Between 1900 and 1970 little change had occurred in the earnings relationships of men and women in employment.

Table 3:3   Median weekly earnings of full-time male and female
             manual workers

Date	Men £ per week	Women £ per week	Women as a percentage of men
1906	1.33	0.66	50.2
1938	3.40	1.61	47.4
1960	14.17	7.58	53.5
1968	22.40	10.80	48.2
1970	25.60	12.80	50.0

Although, as Table 3:3 shows, the weekly earnings relationship
remained steady, the hourly and weekly basic wage rate differential between men and women has narrowed to some extent.
Table 3:4 shows the extent of this trend over the period 1950–71.

Table 3:4   Indices of basic weekly and hourly wage rates

Date	Index of weekly rates		Index of hourly rates	
	Males	*Females*	*Males*	*Females*
October 1950	100	100	100	100
October 1955	138.3	137.4	138.5	137.7
October 1960	169.3	170.5	174.6	174.6
October 1965	207.3	213.0	225.2	231.3
October 1970	280.4	284.8	310.7	316.4
October 1971	312.5	329.7	347.1	367.0

Source: Office of Manpower Economics Report

Thus, while the differential between men's and women's basic
rates has reduced this has not been reflected in the actual take-
home pay of men and women. Higher levels of overtime worked
by men and the impact of additional male increments or rates
negotiated at local level have effectively eroded any advance which
women have achieved in respect of relative wage rates.

This suggests that despite the Equal Pay Act male employees
appear likely to retain their long established earnings advantage
to some degree, and that male average earnings will remain
considerably higher than those of women even after 1975.

The relative pay situation of men and women in 1970, when the Equal Pay Act was passed, could be summarized as shown in Table 3:5.

Table 3:5   Male and female rates of pay in 1970

	Basic pay	Basic pay + overtime pay	Basic pay + overtime pay + shift and other premium payments	Total pay
	£	£	£	£
Manual				
Men	18.5	22.9	23.7	26.8
Women	11.0	11.5	11.7	13.4
Women's pay as per cent of men's	59.5	50.2	49.4	50.0
Non-manual				
Men	32.7	33.7	33.8	35.8
Women	17.2	17.4	17.5	17.8
Women's pay as per cent of men's	52.6	51.6	51.8	49.7
All employees				
Men	23.6	26.8	27.4	30.0
Women	15.1	15.4	15.5	16.3
Women's pay as per cent of men's	64.0	57.5	56.6	54.3

Source: Office of Manpower Economics Report, Table 5, p55

PROGRESS TO DATE

Sections 9 (1) and 9 (2) of the Equal Pay Act gave the Secretary of State for Employment powers to ensure orderly progress towards equal pay by requiring that, by 31 December 1973, women's rates of pay should be not less than 90 per cent of the men's rate where this rate is equivalent as defined in the Act. In 1971 the then Secretary of State for Employment in the Conservative government, Mr Robert Carr, commissioned the Office of Manpower Economics to undertake a comprehensive survey of the progress that had been made by industry and commerce in moving towards equal pay.

The Office of Manpower Economics (OME) consulted fully with the CBI and TUC in drawing up the survey which covered progress at both industry and company level and included the blue- and the white-collar areas. The size of the sample was large, covering 230 national agreements and wages council orders and 145 company agreements.

An additional survey was undertaken of about 200 small companies with less than 100 employees. These companies were not subject to national collective bargaining or wages council orders and might expect to be little affected by the Equal Pay Act.

FINDINGS OF THE OFFICE OF MANPOWER ECONOMICS SURVEY

The principal findings of the OME survey may be summarized as follows:

1 Industry level

The survey was at its most comprehensive in examining progress in industry-wide national agreements. It found that in about one fifth of the national agreements and wages council orders covering manual workers, discrimination in rates of pay had been removed or a commitment had been agreed for its phased removal by 1973 or earlier. In the great majority of these agreements, the percentage differential between the rates of pay for men and women had been reduced to some extent by the award of larger or at least equal increases to women This was a reversal of previous practice and about a third of all women covered by such national agreements and wages orders had benefited. The survey also found that where distinct progress of this sort had been made, it was more marked in the services sector than in manufacturing industry.

At the other extreme the survey reported that about one in nine women manual workers were covered by agreements or orders in which no move had been made towards equal pay and where the women's minimum rates were still less than 80 per cent of the men's.

As far as non-manual workers were concerned, the report noted that all but two of the agreements considered related to the public sector. These two agreements were in the engineering industry and covered 180 000 women clerical workers and technicians. In the public sector, only the steel industry, among nationalized industries, had not introduced equal pay to its non-manual employees.

Apart from the relatively few national agreements covering white-collar workers, the OME also noted several industries employing large numbers of women where a clear pattern of progress could be identified. 'For example, progress in insurance and banking had been substantial in recent years. The clearing banks and most insurance companies have either already achieved or are in the process of achieving equal pay. But since there are few national agreements, the movement towards equal pay for white-collar workers in the private sector is heavily dependent on developments at company level.'[1]

2   Developments at company level

The OME obtained information from 142 large- and medium-sized organizations. Of these 32 had introduced equal pay for either manual or white-collar employees but only one in ten of the total sample had done so for both categories.

While about one quarter of the remaining companies had prepared plans for introducing equal pay by 1975, over 40 per cent had neither taken action nor had produced any plans to do so. Again, progress was more widespread and comprehensive for non-manual than for manual workers.

The summary of the extent of differentials between men's and women's rates in 1971 given in Table 3:6 is taken from the survey.

Table 3:6   Extent of differentials between men's and women's
             rates in 1971

Percentage ratio of	*Percentage of companies*	
women's minimum rate	*Manual*	*Non-manual*
to men's minimum rate	*per cent*	*per cent*
90 per cent or more	9	20
85–89 per cent	30	28
80–84 per cent	37	35
75–79 per cent	12	9
Under 75 per cent	12	9
	100	100

Source: Office of Manpower Economics Report

The principal reason given by the companies which reported
no action and which had no plans developed was that they were
awaiting developments at national level. Industries mentioned in
this connection were printing, textiles and engineering. However,
a number of the companies claimed that they had little or no
overlap between the work done by men and that performed by
women; they appeared to be unaware of the implications of
section 3 of the Act, which requires the amendment of collective
agreements and pay structures where there are provisions relating
specifically to men alone or women alone (see Chapter 2, page 10).

3 Small companies
In the separate survey of 200 smaller companies with less than
100 employees, the survey found widespread ignorance of the Act
and its implications. Only four of the companies were found to
have plans to introduce equal pay and only one in eight of the
companies considered that the Equal Pay Act would affect them.

Only 13 per cent of those companies had established in any
specific sense a formal pay structure; in the great majority of cases
rates of pay were determined on an individual basis. The OME
commented in its report that 'this raises the question how far the
requirement to remove discrimination from pay structures in
section 3 (4) of the Act will affect small companies of this kind'.

It concluded that 'clearly much depends on how far the small employer knows and understands these implications of the Act; our survey was not reassuring on this score'.[2]

ATTITUDE OF EMPLOYERS' ASSOCIATIONS AND TRADE UNIONS

As has been seen, lack of progress in the larger companies was often governed by the lack of developments in planning for equal pay at national level. Employers' associations differed markedly in the extent to which they had been active in bringing about equal pay. Little evidence was found however of associations deliberately holding back from implementing the Act until the last moment. Delays more usually reflected the complexities of introducing equal pay in the industries concerned.

While favouring a phased approach, the TUC has consistently agreed that the end of 1975 is too long to wait for full implementation. But the degree of priority attached to equal pay by individual unions varies; some were pressing for its introduction in full by 1973 or even earlier, while others appeared to be content to wait until the Act becomes effective at the end of 1975. In some instances the interest in the Act of union officials particularly at company level appeared to be no more than lukewarm, possibly because they were preoccupied with other matters such as the Industrial Relations Act or general wage negotiations.

SUBSEQUENT PROGRESS

Since the publication of the OME report the pace of progress towards equal pay has hastened a little. Between mid 1972 and mid 1973 national agreements incorporating either a phased movement to equal pay or giving larger increases to women than to men have been negotiated for over 750 000 women. Further agreements giving women the same increase as men have been negotiated notably in the engineering industry which covers over 400 000 women manual workers.

The movement in gross earnings of men and women between April 1971 and April 1972 shown in Table 3:7 is based on information about average earnings of men and women provided by the Department of Employment.

Table 3:7   Average gross weekly earnings of full-time adults whose pay was not affected by absence*

	April 1972 £ per week	Increase since April 1971	
		£ per week	percentage
Including overtime			
Males			
Manual	32.80	3.30	11.3
Non-manual	43.50	4.40	11.3
All	36.70	3.80	11.4
Females			
Manual	17.10	1.90	12.3
Non-manual	22.20	2.40	12.1
All	20.50	2.30	12.3
Excluding overtime			
Males			
Manual	27.80	2.80	11.4
Non-manual	42.40	4.40	11.5
All	33.20	3.50	11.6
Females			
Manual	16.50	1.80	12.1
Non-manual	22.00	2.40	12.4
All	20.20	2.30	12.6

* Males 21 years and over, females 18 years and over.

Source: Department of Employment

Evidence for 1970 and 1971 from engineering, food and footwear industries published early in 1973 showed that under these selected agreements in these industries women had received greater percentage increases than their male colleagues although

Table 3:8   Female average gross weekly earnings as percentage
of male earnings

	Including overtime percentage	*Excluding overtime percentage*
Manual	52.1	59.3
Non-manual	51.0	51.8
All	55.8	60.8

Source: Department of Employment

cash differentials had widened when overtime, pay and extra hours
were taken into account.

The conclusion that could be drawn is that some progress has
been made recently towards introducing equal pay but there is
still a need for considerable progress to be made by 1975.

EFFECT OF THE CONSERVATIVE GOVERNMENT'S COUNTER-INFLATION POLICY

Although the Equal Pay Act allows the government to require
industry to introduce 90 per cent of the male rate by the end of
1973, the Conservative government decided not to use these
powers, because of its overriding concern with controlling wage
increases by means of its counter-inflation policy.

However, Stage Two of this policy (covering the period 1 April
1973 to autumn 1973) did have special provisions to encourage
progress towards equal pay.

In Stage Two increases in wages were to be strictly controlled.
The main emphasis was on controlling collective agreements. The
rules were that a group of workers could have only one pay increase
in 12 months; there was a limit on the total amount of money
which could be given to a group as an increase (it was £1 per head
per week plus 4 per cent of the average pay bill per head—
excluding overtime—over the previous 12 months); this total
increase could be divided among individual workers in the group

in any way but no individual was to have an increase of over £250 per year.

The equal-pay concession in the rules was that the '£1 plus 4 per cent' limit could be exceeded in order to reduce an existing differential between men's and women's rates by up to one third. No increase outside the pay limit was allowable however if any other increase affecting the group concerned had the effect of widening the percentage difference between men's and women's rates in question.

These provisions appear to have given an additional impetus to establishing equal pay although earnings information is not yet available to confirm this impression.

REFERENCES

1.   OME Report, p.23, paragraph 68.
2.   OME Report, p.27, paragraph 90.

4

Effect of the Act on company payment structures

In the previous chapter reference has been made to section 3 of the Equal Pay Act. This section gives the Industrial Arbitration Board powers to amend both collective agreements and payment structures after 1975 where they specify provisions currently 'applying specifically to men only or to women only' (section 3 (4)(a)). It is now generally understood that where a collective agreement specifies men's rates and women's rates, it must be amended and the women's rates raised to the appropriate male rate. (This is examined in more detail in Chapter 7.) However, it is not as well known that the same should apply to an employer's pay structure which is defined as 'any arrangements adopted by an employer which fix common terms and conditions of employment for his employees or any class of his employees, and of which the provisions are generally known or open to be known by the employees concerned' (section 3(6)).

Thus, even where the terms and conditions of women workers are not covered by a collective agreement but where separate pay scales for men and women doing a similar class of work are established by an employer, the effect of the Act is clear. After 1975 the scales should no longer distinguish between the sexes and the lower women's scales must be eliminated 'in such a way as not to make the terms and conditions agreed for men . . . less favourable in any respect than they would have been without the amendments' (section 3 (4)(b)). In other words the women's structure must be raised to the level of the men's.

Thus, where rates of pay are not determined by a collective agreement and where no job evaluation exists and where there is no identical or overlapping work done by men and women, the Equal Pay Act will still have an effect if pay structures exist for a common class of employee. For example, a company may have established a pay structure for its clerical employees comprising three male salary ranges and two female salary ranges as shown below:

Grade	Male	Grade	Female
A	£1000–1400	D	£800–1000
B	£1250–1750	E	£900–1200
C	£1600–2000		

After 1975 such a distinction between men and women would have to be eliminated and the salary ranges for Grades A and B applied to the women in Grades D and E. The increases to the women concerned and the costs to the employer would be considerable if no phased timetable had been worked out for introducing such a change.

WORK OF THE SAME OR BROADLY SIMILAR NATURE

The Equal Pay Act requires employers to give equal treatment as regards terms and conditions of employment to men and women who are employed on 'like work', which it defines as work done by women which is 'of the same or a broadly similar nature' (section 1(4)) to that done by men. As has been described in Chapter 2, the precise definition of what work is 'broadly similar' is difficult to pin down. The Department of Employment in its publication *Equal Pay—A Guide to the Equal Pay Act 1970* gives the following example of how this provision may be applied:

> Suppose there are two jobs X and Y in an establishment. Men only are employed on job Y. Men and women are employed interchangeably on job X. The men on job Y are paid more than the men on job X. In this situation a woman employed on job X has a claim to equal treatment with the men employed on job X on the grounds that she is doing the same or broadly similar work.
>
> But, in the circumstances described, she has no claim under the Act to equal treatment with the men employed on job Y. Clearly she is not doing the *same* work as the men on job Y because X and Y are different. But, neither can she claim that she is doing work which is *broadly similar* to that of the men on job Y. This is because the Act provides that two jobs are not broadly similar if the differences between them are of practical importance in relation to terms and conditions of employment.' The differences between jobs X and Y are 'of practical importance in relation to terms and conditions of employment' because the men employed on job Y are paid more than the men employed on job X. Hence a woman on job X cannot claim equal treatment with the men on job Y. (Paragraph 9.)

This example is, however, of limited value. Merely because men earn more money on job Y is no reason for assuming that the work is not broadly similar to that on job X. The example assumes that no job evaluation scheme exists and thus the additional payment to men on job Y may be the result of tradition or negotiating pressures, rather than related to the skill or responsibilities of the work itself. Women may be able to demonstrate that the differences between their work and that of job Y are of minor significance if frequent, or only occur occasionally if of major significance. For example, if the type of machine operated is similar in both cases and the length of training required is the same, then the women may be able to claim that the jobs are broadly similar, even though occasionally the men on job Y have to load heavy trays of parts which they produce on their machines. It seems clear that it will be left to the industrial tribunals to establish the case law in such circumstances, which will define the basic criteria for determining whether the jobs in this example are of a broadly similar nature.

A successful appeal by a woman to an industrial tribunal is likely to have a serious effect upon the existing pay structure in an organization or company of any size. In most companies, the established rates of pay reflect, however imprecisely, the accepted differentials between the various jobs. In the past these differentials will probably have been separate for men and women doing the same class of work. After 1975 a successful appeal by a woman in this situation for equal pay will have wider ramifications than the consequent increase to her pay. Not only will her colleagues doing the same work have to be paid the increase but this action will affect all the existing differentials for work undertaken by women in the company. We must therefore expect that situations will arise where tribunal decisions set up stresses and strains on existing payment structures, particularly in large- or medium-sized organizations where employees have trade union representation. It is also necessary to consider the effect on male workers of a sudden and sweeping series of changes to their established pay relationships with the women workers; a series of changes for which they might be ill-prepared. In such a situation a company could well be faced with a serious industrial relations problem which it may lack the means to resolve easily.

The conclusion is clear. The majority of payment problems in industry concern differentials. The Equal Pay Act is likely to disturb many traditional pay relationships where significant numbers of women are involved. Companies which have not used job evaluation and which are not covered by national collective agreements may consider themselves unaffected by the Act. However, after 1975, the successful appeal to an industrial tribunal by a woman for equal pay could create serious problems for a company which has failed to analyse its situation in detail and consequently has not implemented a phased programme of action to prevent such an eventuality occurring.

IMPLICATIONS FOR MULTI-PLANT COMPANIES

The only restrictive clause in the Equal Pay Act is section 1(2) which enables women to claim equality of treatment with men in the same establishment or in other establishments of the same (or associated) employer where the terms and conditions are the same. This effect of the Act on the multi-plant company is frequently misunderstood for it relates to the controversial question of parity which many multi-plant companies are finding is becoming an important negotiating issue for them.

Across many multi-plant companies inequalities in rates of pay exist not only between men and women but also between men doing identical or very similar jobs. In fact such inequalities are by no means restricted to multi-plant firms but are often to be found in the same factory or location where no rationalization or control of the payment structure has been applied. The purpose of the Equal Pay Act is not to establish equal pay for men in multi-plant companies, or indeed within single-plant companies where variations in pay for like work done by men currently occur. Nor indeed is the Equal Pay Act intended to establish equal pay for women doing like work in multi-plant companies where common terms and conditions do not apply.

The basis of applying terms and conditions across a multi-plant company is therefore of vital importance in this context. Where a multi-plant company has established or negotiated common terms and conditions on a company-wide basis, then women in one plant may well be able to draw comparisons with male jobs in another plant of the same company. However, multi-plant companies which establish or negotiate terms and conditions on a decentralized plant-by-plant basis will not encounter the possibility of female comparisons being made outside the individual plant.

The Department of Employment in its publication *Equal Pay—*

A Guide to the Equal Pay Act 1970 gives the following two examples to illustrate this aspect of the working of the Act:

(i)   Suppose an employer owns three establishments—A, B and C—in different parts of the country. The same job is carried out in all three establishments. In A and B it is carried out by both men and women, in C by women only. If the men in A and B have *the same* terms and conditions of employment, and the women in all three establishments also have *the same* terms and conditions (though less favourable than those of the men), then there are common terms and conditions of employment in the three establishments. In such a case, the women in C (as well as the women in A and B) have a claim to equal treatment with the men in A and B.
(ii)   On the other hand if the men in A and B have *different* terms and conditions of employment and the women in all three establishments also have *different* terms and conditions, then there are *not* common terms and conditions of employment in the three establishments. In such a case, although the women in A can claim equal treatment with the men in A and the women in B can claim equal treatment with the men in B, the women in C *cannot* claim equal treatment with either the men in A or the men in B. (Paragraph 7.)

Where a multi-plant company is under pressure to negotiate common terms and conditions and thereby establish parity of treatment for all male workers, the implications of such a decision on its female employees must be carefully examined. The issue of parity of earnings is assuming greater significance to the male members[1] of many trade unions employed in multi-plant companies. Companies which have hitherto adopted a decentralized policy are reluctant to accede to these pressures as the costs of levelling up male rates of pay are often alarmingly high. Such a reluctance must be greater if large numbers of women are employed on work which is the same as the men's or could easily be regarded as being of a similar nature. Thus, it is likely to be in the interests of such employers to maintain a plant bargaining policy with pay structures established on this basis.

It is worth pointing out the interrelationship of this aspect of the Equal Pay Act and the Industrial Relations Act. The latter lays emphasis on the definition of common-interest groups and the creation of bargaining units for such groups. Where multi-plant companies are reconsidering their industrial relations strategies in the light of this and possibly facing parity claims from male employees in different establishments, they should analyse the whole impact of the Equal Pay Act on any conclusion that they reach. The wider the geographical spread of any bargaining unit established to which common terms and conditions and pay are applied, the greater will be the impact of the Equal Pay Act if there are large numbers of women employees in the group concerned.

The Act does not require employers or associated employers to establish common terms and conditions for all employees. The implications of such a requirement would be enormous. It does require women to have the same terms and conditions as their appropriate male counterparts; thus, if all men in an organization are on identical pay levels as a result of a company-wide job evaluation scheme, then women must be similarly treated. On the other hand, if a multi-plant company establishes its pay on a decentralized basis so that men are paid differently in various parts of the country, then women can only draw appropriate local comparisons with male colleagues; they cannot make such comparisons with women employed by the company in another area and covered by different agreements or pay scales.

NOTE

1. For example, the dispute at the Perkins factory in Peterborough in the summer of 1973, the basic cause of which was a claim by the trade unions for parity with the Massey-Ferguson plant in Coventry (Perkins is a subsidiary of Massey-Ferguson).

5

Using job evaluation

The Equal Pay Act gives legislative recognition to the technique of job evaluation. Section 1(5) of the Act states:

> A woman is to be regarded as employed on work rated as equivalent with that of any men if, but only if, her job and their job have been given an equal value, in terms of the demand made on a worker under various headings (for instance effort, skill, decision) on a study undertaken with a view to evaluating in those terms the jobs to be done by all or any of the employees in an undertaking or group of undertakings, or would have been given an equal value but for the evaluation being made on a system setting different values for men and women on the same demand under any heading.

Thus the Act gives considerable emphasis to job evaluation as a means of determining the value of women's jobs relative to those done by men. It goes into some detail implying approval of one particular form of job evaluation—the factor-plan method, which it lays down must not discriminate in the values used between men and women.

However, this section perpetuates a common misconception

about job evaluation, namely that it is a scientific and objective method of measuring the value of a job. Mrs Barbara Castle demonstrated this misunderstanding about job evaluation during the passage of the Act through the House of Commons. It is therefore necessary to examine the basis of job evaluation before considering the implications of the Equal Pay Act on job evaluation.

THE NATURE OF JOB EVALUATION

The most useful analysis of job evaluation is probably to be found in Report Number 83 of the now extinct National Board for Prices and Incomes (NBPI), *Job Evaluation*, which was published in December 1968 (Cmnd 3772). The report defines job evaluation as 'the comparison of jobs by the use of formal and systematic procedures, ie, procedures set down on paper and adhered to as distinct from rule of thumb methods—in order after analysis, to determine the relative position of one job to another in a wage or salary hierarchy'. The main point arising from this definition which should be emphasized is that 'the formal and systematic procedures' can and indeed do vary enormously according to such things as the needs of the situation, the group of jobs being evaluated, advice given to management, the attitude of trade unions and so on. There is no 'correct' system of job evaluation, even though the Equal Pay Act seems to give prominence to the factor-plan method.

The NBPI report states that job evaluation 'is essentially concerned with relationships (between jobs), not with absolutes . . . all job-evaluation methods depend upon a series of judgements. Hence, job evaluation must by its nature contain subjective elements'. Finally, it concludes that 'acceptability is indispensable to a job-evaluation scheme', that is the results must above all be acceptable to those covered by the scheme and those responsible for its administration.

In using the word 'indispensable' to stress the importance of acceptability as a principal criterion of job-evaluation systems, the NBPI could hardly lay greater emphasis on this feature of the technique. Unfortunately the report does not develop this theme but goes on to give a clear description of the principal systems of job evaluation (to which the reader is referred for further information on basic techniques of job evaluation).[1]

It remains to stress what job evaluation can and cannot do. It cannot 'evaluate' the worth of a job in the strict sense of the word, that is give a financial value to a particular job. It does not provide a scientific system of measurement and should never be thought of as having such a capability. It can on the other hand establish the relative importance and worth of a job by reference to its position in relation to other similar jobs. In its simplest form any job-evaluation system can do no more than establish a rank order of a given job population; that is it can provide a list of the jobs in order of their importance. From this rank order further considerations provide the basis of establishing the value of a given job.

The Equal Pay Act gives a different impression of job evaluation. It lays particular emphasis on the factor-plan method of job evaluation and requires those using such a method to ensure that there is no discrimination against women in the design of the factor-plan and points weighting. The Department of Employment's guide elaborates on the reason for this requirement.

> The presumption in the Act is that jobs of different content are evaluated in the terms of the demand which they make on a worker under such headings as effort, skill and so on. There may be discrimination on grounds of sex in the process of evaluation if two jobs, making the same demand in terms of, say, effort, are nevertheless valued differently because one job is carried out by women and the other by men. (Paragraph 12.)

DISADVANTAGES OF THE FACTOR-PLAN METHOD

The TUC fears that a job-evaluation factor plan may be manipulated at the expense of women workers. At a TUC conference in

1973 on progress on the Equal Pay Act a warning was given that undue weight might be given in a job-evaluation scheme to a factor such as physical effort which would benefit male workers in comparison to manual dexterity which would be of greater importance to many jobs undertaken by women. The conference participants were clearly warned what might occur if this happened namely, that women could finish up no better paid than before such a job-evaluation exercise was undertaken if the most important aspects or features of their work are under-recognized by the job-evaluation system.

These fears about the design of a job-evaluation factor plan could be well founded. There is a large amount of subjectivity in the design of such systems and frequently they lack a systematic and cohesive basis. In a previous book[2] I caricatured the design of a factor-plan job-evaluation system as follows:

1   Factors are selected by a group of managers, advised by the personnel manager. He will have chosen a suitable sample from various factor plans of which he has obtained details.

2   Points are allocated to the factors according to the subjective views of the management group ('what we need most from our workforce is high quality work, so obviously "responsibility for the product" must have the most marks.')

3   After prolonged discussion, the points and the definitions of the various levels are agreed for each factor and a sample of 'benchmark' jobs are assessed by the factor plan. When the results are examined, they may well be unacceptable to the assessment panel. The marks for the factors are juggled about, and the benchmark jobs are reassessed until better results ('better' in that they appear more reasonable) are obtained.

4   The factor plan is finalized and the full range of jobs in the population are assessed. Difficulties in ensuring uniform standards of assessment will be encountered, and the assessment panel may revise certain results. Eventually a rank order of jobs is established after a great deal of managerial effort and much time. Then the results are given to the job holders, and all too frequently . . .

5 The job holders reject the results and a long process of consultation and negotiation begins.

UNION INVOLVEMENT IN JOB EVALUATION

The above description only slightly caricatures the factor-plan method of job evaluation. It cannot be gainsaid that some companies have taken great pains with such job-evaluation programmes and have achieved satisfactory results. This has generally been due to two factors:

1 Great care in developing the factor plan and in coordinating the assessments.
2 More important, obtaining the participation and involvement of the job holders and their representatives in carrying out the exercise. This is achieved by getting job holders to complete job descriptions and by including their representatives on the assessment panel.

This participation is crucial in establishing any new wage structure. ('... we ourselves consider that unions should play a part in the establishment of a scheme, for this increases the chance of acceptance'. NBPI, Report Number 83, *Job Evaluation*, chapter 9, paragraph 142.)

But, however much care is taken, the fact remains that the factor-plan system of job evaluation is not only time-consuming but gives a spurious air of objectivity to an intensely subjective matter.

If, as I know from personal experience, there is more than a little truth in this description, the constraints put into the Equal Pay Act to prevent manipulating job-evaluation schemes against women are perhaps necessary, the more so as the TUC and some major unions are ambivalent in their approach to the subject of job evaluation despite the very real opportunities that its use could give women to obtain equal pay. The TUC General Council goes as far as recommending that its use in the equal-pay situation should be treated with caution and concludes that where job-evaluation exercises are undertaken, the unions concerned must be in full agreement with the proposals and method of implementation.

This is an entirely reasonable requirement. The participation and agreement of job holders and their representative organizations is, in my view, crucial to the success of any new wage structure and thus to the implementation of equal pay on a fair and acceptable basis. This emphasis of involvement will be a recurring theme in this book. The implementation of equal pay could prove to be both an expensive and controversial venture for some companies, upsetting established pay relationships and giving an additional impetus to rapidly escalating labour costs.

At company or plant level, therefore, there must be a careful and thorough consideration of the programme of work and methods to be used. The final programme should be based on trade union involvement in the job-evaluation programme for this provides the soundest foundation for success. This involvement in the design of a programme which includes job evaluation should include the full participation of employee representatives in the job-evaluation method used. It provides the best guarantee of ensuring acceptable results and there are systems of job evaluation now developed which are based entirely on establishing a consensus of views about the worth of jobs, which provide one of the most suitable methods of job evaluation for establishing equal pay.

One point should be emphasized. Job evaluation should be seriously considered for any large job population which contains a significant proportion of jobs undertaken by women. While some companies may feel that job evaluation may add to the cost of equal pay, by extending comparisons between men's and women's jobs, this view is not widely held. As the Office of Manpower Economics pointed out in its report, the ramifications of the Equal Pay Act are considerable and job evaluation establishes the whole controversial question of differentials on a defined and systematic basis. Any short-term cost will in most cases be outweighed by the benefits of future stability and of sound and agreed systems.

REFERENCES

1. For a summary of the main types of job evaluation see pp 4–9 of NBPI Report Number 83, *Job Evaluation*, Cmnd 3772, HMSO, 1968.
2. D. T. B. North and G. L. Buckingham, *Productivity Agreements and Wage Systems*, Gower Press, 1969.

6

Paired-comparison method of job evaluation

Chapter 5 has shown that job evaluation can do no more and no less than to establish a rank order of jobs in any given job population. Furthermore the criterion by which any job-evaluation system should be primarily judged ought to be the degree to which its results are acceptable to those concerned with or covered by the evaluation programme. Thus any system should be based on this criterion of acceptability and yet it is curious that until recently job-evaluation methods have not recognized this fact. Certainly any system applied in British industry has had to satisfy certain members of the organization concerned; but more often than not this has been the management and the personnel department. In many cases the systems have been applied to groups of employees without any involvement on their part or of their trade unions. As a result trade unions have tended to regard job evaluation with suspicion, seeing it as a technique which has led to reductions in manpower and to industrial relations problems arising from the fact that evaluation often alters previously accepted differentials. Thus job evaluation has become a frequent subject of negotiation, whereas if it were recognized that the relative worth of jobs can be established most securely and equitably with and by the agreement of the employees concerned, then negotiation on job relationships becomes not only unnecessary but irrelevant. Instead the principal subject of negotiation becomes the payment levels for the jobs as ranked by the evaluation method. However, if this situation is to be reached, the method must be completely open to employees and their trade unions and involve them fully in establishing the rank order of jobs.

PAIRED-COMPARISON METHOD

A number of job-evaluation methods have recently been developed which meet these requirements. They are known by a number of different names, for example, the profile method, direct consensus and paired-comparison method. These various systems differ in detail but they are all based on a number of common and important principles. These are:

1 Acceptability as the sole or principal criterion of the viability of the system.
2 A disciplined method of meeting this criterion by judging jobs in pairs.
3 The full involvement and participation of employees representing the group concerned.
4 Where a factor plan is required, the system allows for the development of a unique set of factors according to the values of the organization and the employees concerned.

PRINCIPAL FEATURES OF THE PAIRED-COMPARISON METHOD

An outline of the paired-comparison method of job evaluation will illustrate how these principles are satisfied in practice. The principal steps in the system are:

1 Agree panel of judges
The basis of this method is establishing a consensus about the

ranking of jobs by a group of representative judges. The method gives considerable responsibility to this panel who should, therefore, be chosen with care. The important qualities of a judge are that he or she should be:

(a) Representative of the group of employees concerned.

(b) Knowledgeable about the job population being evaluated.

(c) Where a union has negotiating rights for the groups of employees, a high proportion of the judges should be shop stewards.

The number of judges is subject to a simple mathematical constraint: the final number selected should divide exactly into the number of jobs in the sample less one (see step 2). In most cases between 10 and 15 judges is an acceptable and convenient number. For example, if there are 37 jobs to be ranked, the number of judges should divide into 36 and a panel of 18, 12, 9 or 6 judges could be used. As will be illustrated later in this chapter, in an equal-pay job-evaluation programme, an equal number of male and female judges should be selected as employee representatives.

2 Select a representative sample of jobs from the job population
The panel undertakes the systematic ranking of a sample of benchmark jobs representative of the whole range of jobs in the population. The final decision on which jobs should be chosen should be taken with the panel and trade union representatives. Again, there is a simple mathematical constraint affecting the decision on the number of benchmark jobs in the sample, namely, that it should be a prime number. A number between 29 and 47 is probably most suitable for a large job population of over 100 jobs and proportionately less where the job population is smaller.

In any programme designed to establish the basis of equal pay, the proportions of male and female jobs should be carefully considered. The purpose of the exercise will be to relate the female jobs to an existing hierarchy of male jobs, and there should be enough male jobs in the sample to reflect the full range of job level and responsibility in the job population. There should be **more** women's jobs than men's jobs in the sample so as to establish a large number of benchmark relationships with the male jobs.

3 Prepare job descriptions and ensure that the judges are fully conversant with all jobs in the sample

For this method of job evaluation, elaborate job descriptions are not necessary. The descriptions should be simple outlines of the principal features, tasks and responsibilities of the job sufficient to serve as an *aide-mémoire* to judges and to assist them in questioning job holders where any judge lacks knowledge about a job in the sample. It is fundamental to the success of this system of job evaluation that all judges fully understand the jobs in the sample. Where necessary interviews and visits must be arranged to enable judges to see the jobs *in situ* and provide them with sufficient knowledge to make their decisions.

4 Judging procedure

When all judges are fully conversant with the jobs in the sample, the panel meets to carry out the assessment procedure. This assessment is made by each judge individually and at this stage privately.

The judges are given assessment forms like that shown in Table 6:1 on which the jobs in the sample are presented in pairs. The forms are prepared so that every possible comparison in the sample is made and the forms distributed so that each judge assesses a proportion of the total number of comparisons. The forms are distributed so that the consistency of any one judge's assessments can be determined.

5 Method of assessment

Each judge is asked to give one of the following scores to each pair of jobs, to reflect his or her judgement of the relative worth or importance of the jobs:

1:9 or 9:1   One job is much more important (worth more) than the other.

2:8 or 8:2 One job is considerably more important (worth more) than the other.

3:7 or 7:3 One job is rather more important (worth more) than the other.

4:6 or 6:4 One job is slightly more important (worth more) than the other.

5:5 The two jobs are of equal importance (equal worth).

Table 6:1 Paired-comparison judging form

Judge A   *Group 1*   *Block 1*   *Number of jobs : 19*

Job No.	Job No.	Job title	Score	Job title
1	2	General shop assistant		Docker
2	3	Docker		Nurse
3	4	Nurse		Miner (underground)
4	5	Miner (underground)		Milkman
5	6	Milkman		Traffic warden
6	7	Traffic warden		Electrician
7	8	Electrician		Policeman
8	9	Policeman		Refuse collector
9	10	Refuse collector		Postman
10	11	Postman		Clerk
11	12	Clerk		Railway porter
12	13	Railway porter		Engine driver
13	14	Engine driver		Shorthand typist pool
14	15	Shorthand typist pool		Taxi driver
15	16	Taxi driver		Typesetter
16	17	Typesetter		Car production worker
17	18	Car production worker		Farm worker
18	19	Farm worker		Teacher
19	1	Teacher		General shop assistant

It is most important not to specify precisely what is meant by 'worth' or 'importance'. This may appear to be naive but, in practice, judges find no difficulty in deciding the relative worth of jobs, provided they are allowed to make their decisions on a total and overall basis and are not restricted by inhibiting definitions that they are required to take into account.

The 5:5 decision indicates a tie and judges should be encouraged to keep such decisions to a minimum. Table 6:2 shows a judging form completed by a judge.

Table 6:2   Completed paired-comparison judging form

Judge A   *Group 1*   *Block 1*   *Number of jobs : 19*

Job No.	Job No.	Job title	Score		Job title
1	2	General shop assistant	2	8	Docker
2	3	Docker	4	6	Nurse
3	4	Nurse	6	4	Miner (underground)
4	5	Miner (underground)	8	2	Milkman
5	6	Milkman	7	3	Traffic warden
6	7	Traffic warden	1	9	Electrician
7	8	Electrician	4	6	Policeman
8	9	Policeman	6	4	Refuse collector
9	10	Refuse collector	6	4	Postman
10	11	Postman	7	3	Clerk
11	12	Clerk	7	3	Railway porter
12	13	Railway porter	2	8	Engine driver
13	14	Engine driver	8	2	Shorthand typist pool
14	15	Shorthand typist pool	6	4	Taxi driver
15	16	Taxi driver	3	7	Typesetter
16	17	Typesetter	7	3	Car production worker
17	18	Car production worker	2	8	Farm worker
18	19	Farm worker	4	6	Teacher
19	1	Teacher	9	1	General shop assistant

Each judge therefore makes individual decisions on the basis described above about the pairs of jobs presented on the ranking form. When the forms have been completed by each judge, they are collected for computation and analysis.

6 *Computation and analysis of results*
The method of scoring described in step five is quite sophisticated and it is necessary to use a computer to analyse the results. In essence the computer does two things:

(a) It produces a rank order for the jobs in the sample by adding together the total decisions of the judges on each job.
(b) It analyses these decisions to establish the consistency of the judge's decisions and the extent of their agreements about the rank order.

This last piece of information—the coefficient of agreement—between the judges is particularly significant. The rank order of jobs produced by using the paired-comparison method (or indeed by any other means) is valueless unless the judges are able to achieve a high degree of agreement about the rank order. If this substantial measure of agreement exists, then the result is most significant. Conversely, a lack of agreement indicates that the judges do not share common values about the worth of jobs in the particular job population. There is now evidence at national, industry, company and plant levels to show that judges usually agree very closely about the importance of jobs. Such agreement is invariably above 80 per cent (0.80) and very frequently above 90 per cent (0.90); this generalization is subject to only one provision, namely that the judges must have a clear understanding of all jobs in the population which they are being asked to assess.

Over the past two to three years this paired-comparison method or one with very similar techniques has been widely used to establish the basis of equal pay for women. In my own company for example, it has been used for all hourly-paid jobs in the factories of the production division and used widely in the clerical, research and development and computer services functions. In all these groups of employees, women employees were either a majority or a very substantial minority. Initially management had some trepidation about the degree of agreement which might exist between male and female judges about the relative importance

and worth of male and female jobs. Such fears were quite unnecessary; in all the job-evaluation exercises undertaken by
panels (and where incidentally women employees had equal
representation with men) a very high degree of agreement was
obtained. For example, four production panels judging hourly-
paid jobs to establish the basis for equal pay of some 7000 employees all produced coefficients of agreement about 93 per cent
(0.93).

This evidence has proved most encouraging as it clearly suggests
that 'agreed' and 'shared' values do exist between men and women
about the relative worth of jobs which in many cases are undertaken by only one of the sexes. Furthermore, the extent of
employee participation in these job-evaluation programmes has
reduced the controversy among male employees over the results.

CASE HISTORY

The following example drawn from my own company's experience
illustrates how the paired-comparison method was used to
establish a job-evaluated basis for equal pay. In one of the northern
locations two factories produced similar products and employ
almost 2000 employees of whom 1150 are women. Wage levels
were negotiated by a joint-negotiating committee and, in 1972, a
long standing job-evaluation system was still in use to establish
the basis for differentials.

Management and trade union representatives were bound to
implement an industry agreement which required equal pay to be
established on the basis of job evaluation. They accepted a joint
recommendation from their parent group's management and
trade union national officers to use the paired-comparison method
of job evaluation, as it was agreed that the existing job-evaluation
method had outlived its usefulness and could possibly discriminate against women employees.

From a total job population of 222 jobs, 37 were selected as the
benchmark jobs for the job-evaluation programme. Out of this

total 18 were male jobs and the remaining 19 were jobs undertaken by women only. Twelve judges were selected to form the panel, of which four were management and supervisory representatives, and eight were employee representatives chosen by the trade union— four men and four women.

Before the panel went through the procedure described earlier in this chapter, they were given some explanation and training in the paired-comparison method. Simultaneously a careful communication programme was undertaken to ensure that all employees covered by the job-evaluation exercise understood the reason why it was being undertaken and the basic method that would be used. As two factories were covered by the exercise, care was taken to ensure that all panel members saw every job *in situ* and talked to job holders, if necessary at considerable length.

These pains taken to ensure that the panel did understand the nature of the benchmark jobs were rewarded when the rank order determined by the judges' decisions was produced. The panel achieved a 94 per cent level of agreement and after a careful discussion of individual decisions which differed from this rank order, were rapidly able to agree to a final order which would provide the foundation for the integrated unisex wage structure.

It had been agreed with the trade union that the job-evaluation programme should not seriously distort the existing male structure of differentials. After discussion with the trade union a ten-grade integrated structure was created and agreed around the rank order of benchmark jobs. The panel was then asked to slot into this structure all remaining jobs using the benchmark jobs as their points of reference. While this part of the exercise may appear to be relatively unstructured, it should be pointed out that the relationships of male jobs to each other and female jobs to each other was already firmly established. These relationships together with the benchmark job rank enabled the panel to make their decisions on 'slotting' the remaining jobs with relative ease. Finally, the results were published and explained to all employees who were given one month in which to appeal to the panel, if any job holder disagreed with the position of his or her job within the structure. Altogether 56 appeals were made and after screening by a small joint sub committee, 19 were referred to the panel for a final decision.

The complete exercise from initial communication and discussion with trade union representatives to the publication of the final wage structure to which all jobs had been allocated was completed within four months and with a minimum of industrial relations problems or administrative difficulties. Both management and the employees and their union appeared to be very satisfied with the result.

CONCLUSION

The system of job evaluation described in this chapter has proved of great value in dealing with the problem of equal pay. As values about the relative worth of male and female jobs appear to be shared by both men and women who are knowledgeable about the jobs in a given population, the paired-comparison method lays emphasis on this consensus of opinion. If such agreement can be obtained, it provides the most secure basis for developing an integrated unisex wages structure, while at the same time it is administratively simple and takes considerably less time than the more conventional factor-plan method.[1]

Should, however, a factor-plan method be required because for example the job population is very large and/or spread over a wide geographical area, then such a plan can be developed by the paired-comparison method.

This method ensures that there will be no argument about the job-evaluation results as far as discrimination on the grounds of sex is concerned.

The Act requires there to be no sex discrimination in the design and implementation of the job-evaluation system used. Where both male and female judges are involved in a paired-comparison job-evaluation exercise and where they reveal a high degree of agreement in their judgements, by definition discrimination cannot be said to exist. There could, however, be grounds for suspecting discrimination if no women are appointed as judges, and this should be borne in mind by any company contemplating the use of the paired-comparison system or a related method to establish the basis of equal pay.

NOTE

1. For further details of this and related systems of job evaluation, the reader is advised to contact either the British Institute of Management or the Institute of Personnel Management advisory services.

7

Effect on collective agreements and industrial relations

In Chapter 2, it was pointed out that the most far-reaching section of the Act is probably section 3 which relates to the revision of collective agreements. This section requires collective agreements and wages councils orders to be amended so as to remove any rates which are defined on the basis of the sex of the worker irrespective of the work or job done. Such amendments must be made to collective agreements (and wages councils orders and employers' pay structures) in order:

(a) To extend to both men and women any provision applying specifically to men only or to women only; and

(b) to eliminate any resulting duplication in the provisions of the agreement in such a way as not to make the terms and conditions agreed for men, or those agreed for women, less favourable in any respect than they would have been without the amendments. (Section 3(4).)

This section has often been misunderstood or appears to have been ignored by many employers and trade unions. Its significance and widespread impact may be appreciated from the following explanation given by the then Under-Secretary of State, Department of Employment to the Parliamentary Standing Committee which was considering the bill in 1970.

> If, for example, a collective agreement lays down for unskilled work a men's rate of 300s. [£15.00] and a women's rate of 240s. [£12.00], under the provisions of the subsection the men's rate must be made to apply to both sexes and to the women's rate also. Under subsection 4(a), there will then be two rates for the same class of work. Paragraph (b) provides for this duplication to be eliminated by striking out the lower rate, with the net effect that the women's rate for unskilled work is raised from 240s. [£12.00] to 300s. [£15.00].
>
> Another type of case would be where a collective agreement laid down a skilled male rate of 400s. [£20.00], a semi-skilled male rate of 350s. [£17.50], an unskilled male rate of 300s. [£15·00], and a women's rate, for all classes of work performed, of 240s. [£12.00]. Under paragraph (a) as drafted, all these rates would have to be extended to cover both sexes. There would then be obvious duplications. The former male rates, relating to skilled, semi-skilled work, would, between them, cover all classes of work in the industry; so would the former women's rate, because it would have been extended from covering all women to covering all workers in the industry. Paragraph (b) then steps in to eliminate the obvious duplication by striking out the lowest rate—the former women's rate of 240s. [£12.00]—with the net effect that skilled women would get 400s. [£20.00], semi-skilled women 350s. [£17.50], and unskilled women 300s. [£15.00].[1]

The Department of Employment's publication *Equal Pay--A Guide to the Equal Pay Act 1970*, gives a further explanation and illustration of the effects of section 3.

> An agreement may lay down a rate of pay for women workers in a particular category and make no provision for men in the same category. The [Board] cannot extend the

scope of a collective agreement to cover men (or women) not, already covered by the agreement. In such a case, therefore a rate 'applying specifically to women only' continues to be required. In these circumstances the [Board] is required to raise the rate of pay concerned to the level of the lowest men's rate in the agreement. (Section 3(4).)

This is illustrated by the following example:

If a collective agreement laid down a skilled male rate of £20.00, an unskilled male rate of £15.00 (but no semi-skilled male rate) and a women's rate (for all classes of work performed) of £12.00, the [Board] would amend such an agreement so that, irrespective of sex, skilled work was paid at the rate of £20.00 and unskilled work at the rate of £15.00. In other words, skilled women workers would be entitled to £20.00 and unskilled women workers to £15.00. The original women's rate—a rate 'applying specifically to women only'—would continue to be required for women employed on semi-skilled work, because there is no category of semi-skilled men provided for in the agreement. In those circumstances, the [Board] would amend the women's rate, which had to be retained from £12.00 to £15.00, namely the lowest rate in the agreement applicable to men. (Paragraphs 22 and 23.)

It should also be noted that similar amendments to collective agreements are going to be necessary where any terms and conditions other than rates of pay currently discriminate between men and women.

PROGRESS TO EQUAL PAY IN 1972

The degree to which section 3 of the Equal Pay Act will affect industries and member companies covered by industry-wide agreements will vary. However, it is safe to say that more women will be covered and therefore affected by this section than any other in the Act.

The report of the Office of Manpower Economics gives the clearest analysis of the picture at industry level. The report was based on an analysis of 182 national agreements and 46 wages councils orders which are on the register of the Department of Employment. The Office of Manpower Economics found that 60 of these 182 national agreements covering manual workers and 1 of the wages councils orders were already either non-discriminating or referred only to men. These 61 agreements covered about 100,000 women employed in male-dominated industries such as mining and quarrying, construction and transport. The report accordingly concentrated its study on the remaining 122 national agreements and 45 wages councils orders which affected almost 3,500,000 women manual workers. This number represents over 40 per cent of the women in employment—a very substantial proportion. The report's summary of the varying degrees of progress made towards equal pay during the two years since the Act was passed up to 31 March 1972 is shown in Table 7:1.

Table 7:1   Movement towards equal pay

Type of agreement	Number of agree-ments	Major Discrimi-nation removed	Phased plan to equal pay	Minor Larger increases to women	Equal increases to women	No movement towards equal pay
Collective agreements	122	8	22	14	41	37
Wages council orders	45	1	1	19	21	3
Total	167	9	23	33	62	40
Per cent of total	100	5	14	20	37	24
Women workers covered (thousands)	3390	224	941	885	632	708
Per cent of total	100	7	28	26	19	21

Source: Office of Manpower Economics Report

It can be seen from this information that in this two-year period there had been no progress at all for over 700,000 women workers —about one fifth of the total number of women covered by the agreements and wages council orders analysed. For an even larger number (over 1,500,000) progress had only been very limited and no plan existed at that time for the removal of discrimination between men and women. On the other hand, 32 agreements covering one third of the total number of women workers had either established equal pay or had specified a specific timetable to establish equal pay.

The Office of Manpower Economics Report also contains a comprehensive analysis of the percentage of the men's rates which women under the agreements and orders currently receive. In particular, the report highlighted three agreements covering large numbers of women where men had received larger increases than women in the period under review. These were hosiery manufacture (Midlands), woollen and worsted manufacture (Yorkshire) and pottery manufacture; a total of almost 120,000 women workers being affected by these three agreements.

Since March 1972 a number of agreements have been concluded which extend the impact of the Equal Pay Act at industry level. As a result, it now appears that over 2,500,000 women workers in the manual and non-manual sectors now have equal pay or are covered by a planned programme to establish equal pay. Other agreements have granted women the same financial increase as men, notably in the engineering industry, where over 400,000 women manual workers received the same increase as male unskilled workers under the agreement reached in 1972. It should be emphasized, however, that equal increases for men and women are not sufficient to comply with the Equal Pay Act. In order to close the gap which exists, these agreements must, within the next two years, provide for larger increases to women than men.

An example from an agreement concluded in 1972 will serve to illustrate the closure of the earnings gap over the period November 1972 to September 1975. This agreement for the paper and paper board making industry is of interest as it covers adjustments to both basic rates and the standard bonus rates for men and women.

The agreement implements the Equal Pay Act in four stages by September 1975. Where men and women do similar work, the women are to adopt the appropriate male classification, for example, skilled, semi-skilled, etc, and will achieve equal pay by means of both general increases and partial consolidation of bonus. Where male and female workers do not do the same work, the female rate is to be compared to the lowest rated male job in the same class.

The following example illustrates how the agreement will be applied:

	Male *£ per week*	*Female* *£ per week*
Basic rate	18.50	14.00
Standard bonus	2.00	3.50
	20.50	17.50

Although there is a gap between male and female basic rates of £4·50 which must be eliminated, there is also a gap—in the women's favour—of £1·50 between male and female bonuses and this must also be eliminated. The method adopted in this industry is a phased reduction of the 'earnings gap' of £3·00 (=£20·50 −£17·50) by adding the following amounts to the female basic rates:

$$1972 \; 30\% \; \text{of} \; £3.00 = \; 90\text{p}$$
$$1973 \; 30\% \; \text{of} \; £3.00 = \; 90\text{p}$$
$$1974 \; 20\% \; \text{of} \; £3.00 = \; 60\text{p}$$
$$1975 \; 20\% \; \text{of} \; £3.00 = \; 60\text{p}$$

$$£3.00$$

At the same time the difference in bonus rates (£1.50) is to be reduced by taking the following amounts from the female bonus rate and adding them to the basic rate (that is, consolidating):

$$1972\ 30\%\ \text{of}\ \pounds1.50 = 45\text{p}$$
$$1973\ 30\%\ \text{of}\ \pounds1.50 = 45\text{p}$$
$$1974\ 20\%\ \text{of}\ \pounds1.50 = 30\text{p}$$
$$1975\ 20\%\ \text{of}\ \pounds1.50 = 30\text{p}$$

$$\overline{\pounds1.50}$$

Thus, by 1975, £4·50 is added to the female basic rate.

The example assumes that any general wage increases given to men during the period will also apply to women in the same class, so that earnings gaps and rates already determined will remain unaffected.

This interesting and carefully designed agreement removes by 1975 both the basic rate differentials which existed between men and women and the higher standard bonus rate which had hitherto applied to women.

REASONS FOR THE SLOW PROGRESS AT INDUSTRY LEVEL

Both employers' associations and certain trade unions are responsible for the slow progress towards equal pay evident in a number of industries. While the Office of Manpower Economics Report acknowledged that some unions had been consistently pressing for the full introduction of equal pay by 1973, other unions were considered to be at the best lukewarm in their attitude to equal pay. 10 per cent of the companies covered by the Office of Manpower Economics analysis claimed that the planned introduction of equal pay 'had been blocked by the attitude of male trade unionists' while in other cases 'men had resisted pay changes which would have narrowed the differentials between themselves and female employees and had successfully demanded the same percentage increases'.[2]

The picture which emerges from the Office of Manpower Economics as far as union attitudes to equal pay is that the TUC has consistently pursued a policy of demanding early implementation of the Act, with varying support from member trade unions at national level but with a majority in agreement with this approach. At local level and in individual plants the trade union attitude is in many cases less positive and in some cases has been positively antagonistic. The changes to established differentials, which the Equal Pay Act will bring about, make such a picture a realistic one. Where opposition does exist at the moment, time and a more thorough and careful explanation to union members and employers should ameliorate the situation.

Employers' associations and their members are shown by the Office of Manpower Economics Report to be, if anything, less positive than the trade union movement, although there are many exceptions. The CBI has been, perhaps understandably, less positive than the TUC in its attitude to equal pay and in its guidance to its members.

REVISING COLLECTIVE AGREEMENTS

In the notes of guidance which it circulated to members on the effect of the Act on industry-wide collective agreements, the CBI distinguished between two separate effects of the Act, namely:

1 The effect on the pay for individual jobs.
2 The effect on the pay levels laid down for occupations or classes of work in such agreements.

As has been discussed, section 3 of the Act gives a procedure for the removal of any differentiation by sex in collective agreements and after 1975 any rate specified for a particular occupation or class of work will have to be universally applicable whether the job is filled by a man or a woman.

The CBI points out that this section of the Act poses serious problems for many industries which use the same broad title for certain male and female jobs, even though the range of jobs performed by the sexes within the scope of this broad classification may be quite different. In such cases, if planned action is not taken before 1975, the legislation could have the effect of raising the pay of many women to the level of the rate or rates laid down in the collective agreement for men, even though the jobs performed by women in the industry concerned may not be the same or broadly similar to those of men in the industry.

The CBI suggests that where this situation exists, agreements should be revised so that rates of pay are based on the content of the jobs rather than on the sex of the workers.

Thus, the CBI proposes that employers should seek to negotiate new job classifications and urges companies to consult together to agree on the terminology to be used. It points out that establishing new job classifications may present problems to some industries where a large number of jobs have to be specified and which have not previously been separately identified in national agreements.

One can envisage serious difficulties being encountered by industries that try to take this advice. It seems certain that all industries will have to merge the minimum rates of pay for male and female unskilled employees, as it is very doubtful if the lowest level of unskilled male job in all industry is dissimilar from the lowest level of female job. If, on top of this identical base rate employers try to erect a new job classification at industry level, they run the risk of causing considerable disruption to existing male differentials in an effort to prevent women in semi-skilled jobs receiving full equal pay.

If, on the other hand, employers merely equate the existing female rate with the unskilled male basic rate (which they are perfectly entitled to do under the Equal Pay Act) a further risk presents itself. A woman in an industry might appeal after 1975 to an industrial tribunal that her job is the same or broadly similar to a semi-skilled male job in the industry for which an industry-wide semi-skilled rate exists. A union might well support such a test case on an industry basis, which if successful could create serious disruption to payment levels across the whole industry.

A delegate at the 1972 women's TUC conference illustrated this situation. 'What is happening now is that if, for instance, there is a man working alongside you in the factory on a capstan machine he is called a capstan operator and you are called a capstan setter operator, so by giving you different designations he is put into a different grade and you find that you are still on the bottom grading'.[3] Should this speaker find, after 1975, that her industry basic rate is that of the unskilled male, it is reasonable to expect her to appeal and with apparently sound grounds that her work is broadly similar to a more highly graded semi-skilled male.

What then is the most sensible approach to this problem of relating the women's rate to the men's in an industry-level collective agreement? The approach to the problem should be an equitable and logical one. Most national agreements specify between one and three basic male rates, perhaps the most common being the latter where unskilled, semi-skilled and skilled rates are frequently negotiated. The fairest and most logical policy in such a situation is to redefine women's jobs in such a way that they can be classified on a similar basis and then to move their rates of pay on a planned basis to the male equivalent by 1975. It is also a simpler policy to implement as most companies should find little difficulty in allocating women's jobs to these categories and reaching agreement on their proposals with the trade unions at national and local level.

This suggested approach is the most simple of the options available at industry level and would have no direct effect upon existing male differentials. However, national agreements are nothing if not notable for their variation.

CASE HISTORY: THE TOBACCO INDUSTRY AGREEMENT

A quite different approach to the Equal Pay Act was adopted by the National Joint Negotiating Committee for the tobacco industry, which provides an interesting contrast with the example previously quoted.

The tobacco industry is dominated by a small number of large employers who having examined the effect of the Equal Pay Act upon their situation came to the following conclusions:

1 The Act would have a significant effect upon each employer, as at least 50 per cent of their manual workers were women.

2 An agreed programme and timetable for establishing equal pay would be of mutual benefit, ensuring that individual employers did not create industrial relations problems by planning different methods and timing.

3 Any national agreement should be based on the continued use of job evaluation to which all major employers were already committed.

Following full and detailed consultation among themselves, the employers proposed to the six trade unions on the NJNC that a joint working party be set up to produce the basis of an agreement. The trade unions agreed to this proposal which was made in 1970 within a few weeks after the Equal Pay Act received the Royal Assent.

By December 1970 the joint working party had reached complete agreement on the basis for implementing equal pay for manual workers in the tobacco industry. The principal features of the proposed agreement which was ratified by both sides early in 1971 were:

1 Full equal pay for work of equal value would be implemented in the industry during 1975. This required all major employers to use job evaluation for determining equal pay.

2 The adult age for both male and female employees to be established at 20 years by 1974. This had been one of the most controversial proposals put forward by the employers. At the time, the age at which the adult rate was paid to women was 18 while for men it was 21. The employers argued that to lower the male adult age during the same period that equal pay for work of equal value was being implemented would produce unacceptably high costs to the employers. The trade unions were reluctant to agree to the employers' proposal but finally agreed when examples of the effect of lowering the male adult age were considered in detail (this aspect of the Act is considered in more detail in the following chapter).

3   Timetable.

Stage 1—1971
During this year all employers undertook to pay equal cash increases to men and women. (It should be noted that only minimum earnings levels are negotiated at national level in this industry; wage increases are agreed and implemented at company level.) During Stage 1 employers undertook to re-examine their job-evaluation schemes to ensure that no discrimination existed between the sexes. As a result, at least two large employers undertook a new re-evaluation programme.

Stage 2—1972
1   Age at which the adult rate paid to women raised to 19.
2   Male/female differentials to be reduced by one quarter.

Stage 3—1973
1   Age at which the adult rate paid to women raised to 20.
2   Male/female differentials to be reduced by one third.

Stage 4—1974
1   Age at which the adult rate paid to *male* workers reduced to 20.
2   Male/female differentials to be reduced by one half.

Stage 5—1975
Remaining male/female differentials completely removed.

This agreement, it should be emphasized, did not set out the minimum rate of progress for the industry, but the timetable with which all employers and trade unions had to comply. However, within each calendar year, employers and trade unions at company level could agree the actual date at which each stage took effect.

Table 7:2 illustrates how this agreement works in practice.

Table 7:2 Increases to female wage scales

Age	1971 rates			1972		1973		1974		1975	
	Male £	Female £	Differential £	Equal pay increase	Balance remaining	Equal pay increase	Balance remaining	Equal pay increase	Balance remaining	Equal pay increase	Balance remaining
15	15.00	14.00	1.00	0.25	0.75	0.25	0.50	0.25	0.25	0.25	—
16	16.50	15.50	1.00	0.25	0.75	0.25	0.50	0.25	0.25	0.25	—
17	18.00	17.00	1.00	0.25	0.75	0.25	0.50	0.25	0.25	0.25	—
18	19.50	18.50	1.00	0.25	0.75	0.25	0.50	0.25	0.25	0.25	—
19	21.00	18.50	2.50	1.37½*	1.12½	0.37½	0.75	0.37½	0.37½	0.37½	—
20	22.50	18.50	4.00	1.37½*	2.62½	1.37½*	1.25	1.37½*	1.37½†	1.37½	—
21	24.00	18.50	5.50	1.37½	4.12½	1.37½	2.75	1.37½	1.37½	1.37½	—

* Increases greater than agreed formula to ensure:

1 Common rate for all females 19 and over in 1972.

2 Common rate for all females 20 and over from 1973.

† Male rate increases to £24.00.

The agreement was widely publicized to all hourly paid employees in the industry through a jointly agreed explanatory leaflet which was distributed to each of the approximately 30,000 manual workers in the industry (a copy of this leaflet is given in the Appendix).

The tobacco industry is now half-way through its staged programme of implementation. It has provided the industry, the trade unions and its women workers with a comprehensible, planned and equitable basis for implementing the Equal Pay Act and remarkably few problems have been encountered in applying it. The agreement represents a substantial potential increase in employment costs for employers which, however, they have had time to plan and to minimize by programmes of productivity improvements and, where appropriate, capital investment. The trade unions have faced criticism for allowing the age at which the adult rate is paid to be raised to 20, but know that they will have established one of the most comprehensive and equitable equal-pay programmes in private industry by 1975. Both sides of the industry have cooperated in drawing up and implementing the agreement which is based on the use of job evaluation as the basis of sound wage administration. Neither the employers nor the trade unions wished the Equal Pay Act to prejudice the continued use of this technique and accordingly incorporated its use into their national agreement.

REFERENCES

1. *Minutes of Proceedings on the Equal Pay (Number 2) Bill. Standing Committee H* (House of Commons Paper, Session 1967–70, Number 205), HMSO, 1970, Cols 275–6.
2. OME Report, p.29, paragraph 98.
3. Mrs I. Money, AUEW Women's TUC Conference, 1972.

8

Effects on terms and conditions of employment

The Equal Pay Act does not only apply to wages, salaries and rates of pay. It also covers all other terms and conditions of employment, except those conditions which relate to retirement, marriage, death or maternity provisions or which arise from compliance with part 6 of the Factories Act 1961.

FACTORIES ACT RESTRICTIONS

The Factories Act places certain restrictions on the employment of women who do manual work in factories. Women must not work for more than 48 hours in each week. Work must not commence before 7 am or end after 8 pm (1 pm on Saturday). Women workers must be given a rest interval of at least half an hour after $4\frac{1}{2}$ hours of continuous work, while overtime should not exceed 6 hours in any week or 100 hours in any year. It is, of course, possible for an employer to make an application for exemption from these provisions, but if the application is not made jointly with the trade union which represents the women concerned, then the Department of Employment must arrange to consult with them, to obtain their agreement in effect before granting such an exemption.

There has been some pressure from employers for the majority of such restrictions to be abolished on the basis that if women are to enjoy the benefit of equal pay, then it is only reasonable for them to receive the same treatment as their male colleagues. The trade unions have not been entirely opposed to considering such a move, but have insisted on full consultation if such changes are contemplated. The trade union movement has, in effect, the right of veto as legislation stands at present and are reluctant to lose this power.

One might venture to suggest that the current limitations on women's hours of work are a reasonable precaution taken by a society which should show some concern for the woman's role as a mother and, dare one suggest it, as a wife. A large proportion of working women have a dual role and a very exhausting one it often is. Thus, the current legislation justifies itself and its continued existence in no way militates against women's right to equal pay. Conceivably it has more bearing on the question of equal opportunity.

Thus, as the Department of Employment's publication *Equal Pay—A Guide to the Equal Pay Act* points out, 'so far as the terms and conditions of a woman's employment are affected by compliance with the law regulating the employment of women . . . the Act does not require the equal treatment of men and women' (Paragraph 43).

PENSIONS

The Equal Pay Act does not require equal treatment where women may enjoy special terms and conditions of employment in connection with the birth of a child or with retirement, marriage or death. Retirement includes retirement 'whether voluntary or not on grounds of age, length of service or capacity' (section 6(2)).

Thus an important group of an individual's terms and conditions are excluded from the provisions of the Equal Pay Act. The most significant are those concerned with pensions. It is well known that the TUC pressed Mrs Barbara Castle very hard to include pension rights in the Equal Pay Act. It has been reported that after the Bill had completed its committee stage and was having its third reading, in the House of Commons, the TUC succeeded in persuading Mrs Castle to include a provision that a woman should have the same pension rights (including a right to join an occupational scheme) as men doing the same or similar work. However, it apparently proved to be too complicated and time consuming to introduce the necessary amendment in the House of Lords and so when the Act became law pension rights were not included.

Comprehensive changes to current pension legislation are at the time of writing before Parliament. The Conservative government's Social Security Bill includes important provisions which affect the entitlement of women in employment to a pension. The consideration of these proposals is outside the scope of this book, but one point is worth making. The Conservative government's proposals do not include any change in the pensionable age; that is the age at which a government pension is paid. This will remain at 65 for men and 60 for women and so one of the most significant differences in the conditions of employment between men and women will remain.

COMMON DIFFERENCES IN TERMS AND CONDITIONS

What then are the more important terms and conditions of employment which must be made equal under the Equal Pay Act? Certain conditions of employment have always been the same for men and women. These include overtime and shift premia, holiday entitlements and the length of the working week. However, variations often exist in the following:

1 Long-service pay
These differences have been a reflection of male/female pay differentials and will need to be equalized.

2   *Sickness and absence payment schemes*

As such schemes are generally related to actual payment levels, they have naturally reflected differences in pay between men and women. However, discrimination has also existed in the qualifying periods of service required before an employee is entitled to benefits under such a scheme. Thus schemes exist where male employees with one year's service qualify for sick pay but women have to have five years' service. Such differentials will have to disappear under the terms of the Equal Pay Act.

3   *Adult age*

Perhaps the most important difference in conditions of employment between men and women is the age at which the adult rate is paid. This is of particular significance to manual workers where for many years male workers have been paid the full adult male rate at 21 whereas women have achieved the female adult rate at 18.

AGE AT WHICH ADULT RATE IS PAID

In the last three or four years, trade unions have begun to succeed in reducing the age at which men receive an adult rate to 20 or 18 years of age. This process has of course been hastened by pressures from other legislation. For example, the 18-year-old is now entitled to vote, and as a result 18 is increasingly seen as the age at which adulthood is achieved.

However, in much of industry the age at which the adult rate is paid remains at 20 or 21 for men. The Equal Pay Act requires this age to be the same for men and women by the end of 1975 and at first sight the obvious step is to reduce the male age from 21 or 20 to 18 perhaps over a two- or three-year period. The cost implications of such a move however can be very heavy for any company employing large numbers under 21 years of age. The following example will illustrate the effect on women's rate of pay of not reducing the adult age for men from 21 to 18.

1972 weekly rates for a job rated as the same or equivalent:

	Men	Women
At age 21	£28	£19.60
At age 18	£21	£19.60

In this example, if women are to receive equal pay by 1975 in three equal stages, then the pay for a 21-year-old woman would be increased by three equal-pay supplements of $\frac{1}{3}$ (£28.00 − £19.60) = £2.80 per week in 1973, 1974 and 1975. A girl aged 18 in 1972 is entitled to increases of only $\frac{1}{3}$ (£21.00 − £19.60)=46.6p per week each year. However, she will receive a 21st-birthday increase in 1975 of £7 per week. A girl aged 18 in 1975 would earn £21. By maintaining at 21 the age at which adult rates are paid, the company saves up to £7 a week on every employee aged under 21. (General increases in pay levels are assumed to affect all rates proportionally and have been ignored.)

Of course it can, and indeed will, be argued by the trade unions that now that society has established adulthood at 18, both male and female employees should receive the adult rate at 18. However, at a time of strong inflationary pressures and where a company is faced with substantial equal-pay costs, the additional cost of a reduction in the adult age may be too great to bear. In one company for example, the cost of introducing equal pay was accurately estimated at 17 per cent of the total wages bill and a reduction in the adult age would have added a further 5 per cent to this figure.

In addition, a reduction in the age for the adult rate when equal pay is also being introduced produces very high increases for certain girls, as the following example will demonstrate:

Rate for equivalent jobs

Age	Men	Women
21	£28	£20
20	£26	£20
19	£24	£20
18	£22	£20
17	£20	£18
16	£18	£16

In this example, if one assumes that an adult male would only receive a £2 per week general increase per year the girl who is under 18 years of age by contrast receives during a calendar year:

> £2 per week general increase
> £2.65 equal pay supplement
> £2 per week age increase in moving say from the 17-year-old scale to the 18 year scale.
> *Total* £6.65 per annum.

If, however, the age for the adult rate rises each year to 21 the girl forgoes her age scale increase and receives the £4.65 increase like her older female colleagues.

This, as explained in Chapter 7 was the type of agreement reached by the tobacco industry NJNC in its national agreement on equal pay. Of course, one cannot expect the adult age to remain permanently at 20 or 21 years of age. But if it is established at 20 or 21 while equal pay is being introduced, then the costs of reducing the age to 18 can be delayed and spread over a period after 1975 when the industries affected are more capable of absorbing the additional cost involved.

ABSENCE AND LABOUR TURNOVER

Those who oppose the concept of equal pay sometimes argue that equal pay should not be introduced because it will result in labour costs which industry will have to bear. This point of view is never, to my knowledge, based on claims that women are less productive or hardworking in their jobs than the men, but rather it is based on the levels of female absence and labour turnover compared with those of men in jobs of similar level.

For example, if female absence levels are higher, then it is due to the boring routine and repetitious jobs which is all that industry is prepared to offer women. Certainly there is evidence that women are more frequently absent than men in similar levels of manual work (an example from my own company is given later in this chapter). But undeniably, as, for example, Baroness Seear has cogently argued, the vast majority of women at work are to be found 'mainly near the bottom of the occupational ladder',[1] and employers do far too little to use and develop the skills and abilities of their female employees.

While it is generally agreed that labour turnover among women is higher than among men, those in favour of greater equity and opportunity for women claim that the statistics mask the relative stability and loyalty of the married woman who returns to work after her family responsibilities have diminished. Proponents of this argument can produce substantial evidence to support their claim.[2]

In this controversial area what view should the practising manager adopt and what effect will the Equal Pay Act have on the situation? First—he would be well advised to examine the present facts of the situation which, if available, may serve him as the best basis for reaching a conclusion. For example, between 1970–72 the comparative absence and labour turnover statistics for the manual workers of one company employing nearly 2,000 employees, of which 55 per cent were women were as follows:

	1970		1971		1972	
	Labour turnover	*Absence*	*Labour turnover*	*Absence*	*Labour turnover*	*Absence*
Men	28.1%	5.5%	20.1%	5.6%	14.3%	5.4%
Women	37.4%	9.3%	31.0%	10.6%	23.8%	9.8%

The men and women concerned in the example were doing a roughly similar level of work and enjoyed, irrespective of sex, the same generous absence-payment scheme, which included a measure of self certification in certain circumstances. From such information only one conclusion can be drawn; in this particular company female absence and labour turnover greatly exceeded those of the men. The costs therefore of recruitment and absence cover for women in an equal pay situation will be greater than for a similar group of men.

These are not, of course, the only factors to be taken into account when assessing the relative costs of employing men and women. What are the productivity levels of the women in the factory? Can they be trained more quickly than men? Are many or some of the jobs performed better by women than men? Obviously it is difficult to produce accurate assessments of the comparative costs of using male and female labour. Certainly no manager should use such calculations as a reason for avoiding implementation of the Equal Pay Act—quite apart from the legal sanctions and consequent problems involved. Rather he should see what opportunities the Equal Pay Act offers him to reduce the extent of absence and labour turnover among his female employees.

At this point it is necessary to separate the two subjects that until now have been linked, as it is likely that the Equal Pay Act will have a different effect upon each. If a manager implements the Equal Pay Act fully, particularly on the basis of equal pay for work of equal value, he may expect his rates of pay to be very competitive in the local labour market and this fact should tend to reduce labour turnover. Women will be less likely to leave for other employment in the area and this element in labour turnover should therefore diminish.

Absence levels however may well increase particularly if a pay-related absence-payment scheme is in existence. In any event it is not unreasonable to suppose that women may have a similar attitude to the miner who was asked why he only worked four days a week. 'Because I don't earn enough in three' was his reply. Many women, especially those that are married with home and family also competing for their attention, will not unnaturally sometimes take this view and act upon it. So, particularly, if the jobs that the women do are uninteresting, absence levels as a result of equal pay may well increase.

The manager therefore needs to consider both these aspects of the employment of women as a result of the Equal Pay Act. The Act will give him the opportunity, if he takes it, to attract a greater number of female applicants and to retain them in his employment. However, women's absence levels may increase as a result of higher pay and he should give attention therefore to methods of reducing absence levels. Accurate statistics on absence levels and trends should be developed and the attention of management and supervision focused on the control of absence levels. Standards of attendance should be established and discussed with the trade unions and employee representatives concerned. Company medical and welfare departments can make an important contribution in this area in counselling employees who develop a regular pattern of short-term absence and in seeking the cooperation of doctors and medical authorities in the area.

REFERENCES

1. Nancy Seear, 'The position of women in industry', in *Two Studies in Industrial Relations* (Research Paper Number 11, Royal Commission on Trade Unions and Employers' Associations), HMSO, 1968.
2. ibid.

9

A planned strategy for implementing equal pay

Any company which employs a substantial proportion of women needs to give the most careful consideration to the effect that the Equal Pay Act will have. A recent Department of Employment publication 'Equal pay—half time checklist' pointed out that industry and commerce had been given a transitional period of over five years to plan for the introduction of equal pay. This transitional period had been allowed, said the Department, because equal pay 'can vitally affect':

Labour costs
Pay structures
Production methods
Industrial relations arrangements

To this list might be added:

Manpower planning
Organization and methods

The Department of Employment's concern at the extent of

D

progress to date is shown by its decision to publish a booklet at this time emphasizing that employers should not assume that the Equal Pay Act does not affect them.

Those companies which have not yet worked out their policy on equal pay need to give the matter urgent consideration. A company strategy must be based upon a careful and comprehensive analysis of the likely effects and implications of the Act.

In companies of any substantial size, that is with more than 1,000 employees, a management working party may be an appropriate vehicle to carry out such an analysis. I was chairman of such a working party set up in 1970 with the following terms of reference:

> To investigate the implications of introducing equal pay into the company in relation to the timetable of the Equal Pay Act. This investigation should specifically examine the likely effects of equal pay on company costs, wage and salary administration and industrial relations.
>
> In the light of this study, recommendations should be made on implementing equal pay in accordance with the Act's timetable at the minimum cost reconcilable with the maintenance of good employee relations and defined wage and salary administration. In preparing these recommendations, the working party should pay particular attention to manpower planning and the rate of technological change in the company.

With these terms of reference the working party's membership was selected to provide the necessary expertise to meet the terms of reference, which the working party had been given. Thus, as well as representatives of the personnel department who had functional responsibilities for employee relations, remuneration planning and training, other members brought experience of line management in production and distribution (which were the largest employers of women in the company) of development engineering and of financial analysis.

NATIONAL AGREEMENTS

The effect of any national agreement on a company's situation will normally be the first thing to be considered. National agreements are important because after 1975 as has already been described in Chapter 7, the minimum rates of pay laid down for men in such agreements must be applied to women.

Thus, any company covered by a national agreement should pay particular attention to the effect of the agreement on the rates of pay which their women employees will receive after 1975. Where necessary, detailed discussions with staff of the employers' association will assist a company to clarify the details of any current agreement and the likely or planned changes which will occur by 1975.

WAGE, SALARY AND MANPOWER ANALYSIS

Unless companies have detailed and accurate information about their employees and what they are paid, meaningful conclusions about the effect of the Equal Pay Act are impossible to draw.

The rates of pay and weekly or hourly earnings excluding all shift or overtime premia should be taken out and analysed over a typical reference period. The Conservative government's pay policy which requires companies under Stage Two to establish the annual pay bill for all groups of employees will have given an impetus to companies to carry out this analysis,

On the basis of accurate wage and salary information the cost of introducing equal pay can be accurately analysed and assessed. In order to produce accurate estimates certain assumptions need to be made, notably:

(*a*) The percentage rise in male earnings up to and including the year 1975.

(*b*) That for the purpose of the analysis, there will be no changes in the numbers employed nor will the ratio of men and women change significantly.

On the basis of such assumptions, a cost analysis on the following lines can be carried out so as to provide an accurate estimate of the costs involved:

1 Establish the groups of male employees to which female employees will relate for equal pay purposes, for example, hourly-paid manual workers, clerical employees, factory supervision, etc.

2 Establish the ratio of men and women in each of the 'common-interest' groups identified under item 1 above.

3 Analyse the earnings of men and women in each reference group over a sample period of one to three months. This information should exclude all premiums such as overtime and shift allowances.

4 Assess the general relationship of male and female jobs in each common-interest group unless job evaluation already applies. If this is the case, the precise relationship of female jobs to male jobs in each wage and salary structure will be known. In the absence however of such comparative information, best assumptions must be made on how women's jobs will relate to men's. This requires an analysis of rates of pay and job content so that reasonably accurate comparisons can be made.

5 Calculate the increase in male earnings up to and including 1975 (see assumption (*a*) above.)

6 Determine annual cost of equal pay, based on the known or assumed speed of attaining equality of earnings, that is, is the company going to wait until the end of 1975 to establish equal pay or if not, what date will it set for reaching this position?

Tables 9:1 and 9:2 illustrate this costing procedure.

Table 9:1   Manpower Analysis—Ratios of Males to Females

(a) *Manual workers*	*Numbers*		*Ratio*		
	Males	*Females*	*Males*		*Females*
Factory A	756	1 817	1	:	2.4
Factory B	392	749	1	:	1.9
Factory C	551	270	1	:	0.5
	1 699	2 836	1	:	1.7 approx
(b) *Staff*					
Location A	280	180	1	:	0.6
Location B	340	316	1	:	0.9
Location C	187	891	1	:	4.8
	807	1 387	1	:	1.7 approx

On the basis of these numbers and ratios a cost analysis of payroll increases between 1973 and 1975 might produce the following, assuming that male rates of pay increase by 7 per cent cumulative per annum over the period and that in 1973 women were paid on average 85 per cent of the men's rates of pay.

Table 9:2   Cost analysis of payroll increases between 1973 & 1975

	1973 £ 000	1974 £ 000	1975 £ 000
Male increases			
Manual workers	178	190	206
Staff	113	121	129
Female increases			
Manual workers	252	286	323
Staff	165	187	211
Female equal pay supplement			
Manual workers	230	241	264
Staff	148	160	169
Total	1 086	1 185	1 302
Add current payroll	10 136	11 222	12 407
Projected payroll	11 222	12 407	13 709
Percentage increase	10.7	10.6	10.5

Thus on the basis of both the numbers and ratios of men and women shown in Table 9:1 and the assumptions given, this analysis shows that payroll costs will increase from £10,136,000 to £13,709,000 of which £1,212,000 can be identified as the cost of introducing equal pay.

MANPOWER PLANNING, SELECTION AND TRAINING

The cost analysis above has been carried out on the assumption that no changes will take place in the numbers of men and women employed during the period 1973–75. However, the increased costs of introducing equal pay highlight the need for a working party to examine the principal means by which the cost to a company of introducing equal pay may be to some extent absorbed.

This examination should be as accurate and comprehensive as possible. Two major aspects of manpower utilization should be included:

1 Capital investment plans and the impact of technological change. While the main emphasis of such an analysis will almost certainly be in the manufacturing area, the effect of such investment in the clerical and administrative areas should not be ignored. The effect of possible changes, such as computerization, changes to office systems and mechanization, of more efficient telephone equipment etc are relevant in this respect.

2 The introduction of improved methods and the consideration of ways of raising employees' levels of performance. Here again, the range of options is wide. Depending on a company's situation, this might range from the introduction of incentive schemes based on work study in the factory through an intensive method study of production processes to considering applying measurement and accurate work loading to the offices.

In some companies a systematic investigation into current and projected levels of manpower utilization may produce evidence of a dearth of information and highlight the need for a systematic feasibility study in this area. It is sometimes argued that employers have benefited for too long in employing women as a cheap source of labour. To the extent that there is truth in such an accusation, equal pay will compel a more rigorous analysis of the contribution of women to the organization and highlight the need for companies to devote more attention to raising the general level.

In this context it should be noted that equal pay will focus attention on the more fundamental aspect of the way that industry and commerce structure the contributions of their female employees. Although the Equal Pay Act does not cover the question of equal opportunity for women, it creates pressures which will bring this subject more to the forefront of attention. The logical outcome of this trend in society of equal treatment for men and women at work is that there will be a single labour market in which opportunities are open to all, irrespective of sex in the majority of cases and where the prospective employee is judged on ability and experience.

While companies may be hesitant to make too overt a move in this direction, the increasing costs of employing women do highlight the need to enlarge and enrich women's jobs where possible, thereby creating better job and career opportunities for them. In addition, more attention and care will need to be given to the selection and training of women. Such a programme will require the preparation of accurate job descriptions and the introduction of systematic selection methods and properly designed training programmes based on a careful analysis of training needs. While the Industrial Training Act and the training boards have already provided a powerful stimulus to raising selection and training standards, there is some evidence that much of the attention of industry and commerce has been male oriented. For example, the ratios of men and women attending training courses on a 'sandwich' or day-release basis under company sponsorship shows this only too clearly.

One may conclude therefore that the increasing costs of employing women will highlight the need to consider the contributions that they have been traditionally asked to make to industry and commerce. There are those who believe that the effect of the Equal Pay Act will be to reduce the number of jobs for women in the UK, but much will depend on the British economic situation in the next five years. Women represent the principal source of additional manpower which it appears at the time of writing will be needed as the economy absorbs the rapidly reducing number of unemployed and the country strives to maintain a period of substantial economic growth. If such growth can be maintained, the costs of equal pay can be absorbed while maintaining and perhaps increasing the job opportunities for women. If, however, the momentum is lost, it may be that women will feel the effects first.

INDUSTRIAL RELATIONS AND EMPLOYEE ATTITUDES

A systematic analysis by a company of the effects and implications of equal pay should include an assessment of the effect it will have on industrial relations and employee attitudes. While the trade union movement, as has already been discussed, has adopted a generally positive approach to equal pay, the extent to which the male trade union members agree that women warrant equal pay is more open to doubt. When this was suggested by *The Sunday Times*[1] in a series of articles by Vincent Hanna at the end of 1971 (one of which had the somewhat provocative title 'How the shop-floor has betrayed women') the unions' reply was prompt and spirited. For example Marie Patterson, National Women's Officer of the TGWU and Chairman of TUC's Women's Advisory Committee stated unequivocally in the same newspaper that 'I hardly ever come across a male shop steward who does not support a women's struggle—if and when the women themselves are organized and putting up a fight'. This forthright statement only lacked a rider to the effect that this is true provided that the women's struggle is not for pay or opportunity at the men's expense. Few male shop stewards would be prepared to join with their sisters in that sort of struggle.

Some companies may experience opposition from their male employees to the practical implications of equal pay, and if these occur their resolution will depend upon negotiation with predominantly male shop stewards. Two sources of potential difficulty may be the most frequently identified in any industrial relations analysis: first, the attitude of men to changes in traditional differentials and second, the possibility of changes in traditional employment practices.

There is some evidence that equal-pay supplements to women heighten male expectations for wage and salary increases. This has been particularly evident among skilled craftsmen in some process industries where women predominate and the craft unions represent a minority among the manual employees. To reduce such potential pressures, companies are best advised to pay equal-pay supplements at a different time in the year to the general negotiated increase.

A longer-term problem is the effect of equal pay where large numbers of women dominate any group of employees. Evidence from the teaching profession and civil service points to a reduction in the level of male earnings in women-dominated groups. Clearly during the period that equal pay is being introduced, it is in employers' interest from a cost point of view to keep male increases to as moderate a level as can be negotiated. The higher the men's rates of pay are in 1975, the greater the costs of equal pay. However, such a policy can obviously lead to negotiating difficulties if pursued too vigorously by an employer.

Changes in the jobs traditionally done by men and women may be an even more controversial industrial-relations subject created by equal pay. Where through job evaluation or the merging of basic rates jobs done by men and women are similarly paid, pressures will increase to change traditional employment practices. In many organizations jobs are not available to both sexes. It is as rare to find a male private secretary as a female craftsman. While these two particular jobs may remain the traditional preserve of their sex, other jobs until now the exclusive preserve of the male or female may have to be made available to either sex. The low-graded unskilled male worker may demand the opportunity to train for the semi-skilled job traditionally done by women. In staff areas, women may demand wider opportunities in clerical, administrative and related functions, particularly at the more senior levels.

These are some of the industrial-relations problems which may present themselves to companies as a result of a careful and imaginative analysis of the implications of equal pay. They must be carefully considered and management policies and plans made in anticipation.

NEED FOR EFFECTIVE COMMUNICATION

This chapter suggests that many companies can best tackle the problems of equal pay which may face them by undertaking a comprehensive and detailed analysis of the likely effects. A working party drawn from appropriate members of management may be a suitable vehicle for carrying out the work involved. Certainly if the Equal Pay Act is likely to have a substantial impact, its effects require systematic analysis before a programme of implementation is drawn up, discussed and negotiated with the trade unions where appropriate.

Following agreement on this programme, it is strongly recommended that it is fully communicated to the employees concerned. Such a programme will assist in obtaining employees' acceptance and understanding of what is involved and go some way to reduce some of the industrial-relations problems identified earlier in this chapter.

It will also ensure that women in the company understand how equal pay will affect them for there is still much misunderstanding about the concept. For example, one sample survey of 60 women undertaken in 1971 in two locations of a large multi-plant company revealed that 85 per cent of the women felt that equal pay was fair for the same jobs, but had no real understanding of equal value, which they found difficult to envisage in practical terms.

However, this survey showed that the principal reason why

these women went to work was financial, and that other factors such as opportunity, promotion and job security were very much secondary to this. Nevertheless, although the women interviewed said that they worked principally for money, they did not see themselves in any way 'bread winners'. They wanted high wages principally in order to buy extras for themselves or their families and a majority considered their earnings as 'pin money'.

Thus it is probable that even when equal pay is fully implemented, women will continue to view their earnings as supplementary to the men's basic earning responsibility. As equal pay provides higher pay for women, so evidence is beginning to appear that increased leisure is the most important aim of women at work. So conceivably equal pay may increase the pressures already apparent for a reduction in the length of the working week.

REFERENCES

1. *The Sunday Times*, December 1971.

IO

Longer-term effects of the Equal Pay Act

EQUAL PAY AND INCOMES POLICY

In the middle of June 1973, the Department of Employment issued a booklet to 40,000 employers entitled *Equal Pay—What are you Doing about it?* Its date of publication was about half way through the transitional period from the passing of the Act in 1970 to the date (29 December 1975) when the Act comes into effect. The booklet provides a clear checklist of points which employers need to examine if they employ women and contains simple advice on the steps employers should consider if they are to comply with the Act. The booklet is based on the Report of the Office of Manpower Economics study of the progress being made by companies in meeting the Act's requirements and its publication provided tangible evidence that the government was concerned at the extent of the progress during the first two and a half years of the transitional period.

The Act of course gives the Secretary of State for Employment the opportunity to make an order requiring the partial implementation of equal pay by 31 December 1973, if he is not satisfied with the extent of the progress made by that date. However, despite the indication of governmental concern at the rate of progress based on the evidence of the OME Report, the Conservative government has not taken these powers. Its decision was undoubtedly affected by the government's incomes policy which was introduced in November 1972. After the six months freeze, the second phase of the pay policy made specific allowance for progress towards equal pay to be made outside the maximum increase permitted of 4 per cent + £1.00 for each group of employees. Under the pay code, women could receive one third of any differential which existed between their pay and that of comparable male jobs on the 31 December 1973. These concessions under the government's pay policy were a specific incentive to faster progress to equal pay, although their effect was much less than if the government had required women's rates to be brought up to 90 per cent of the men's by the end of 1973.

This intervention by the government, encouraging equal-pay increases within the context of tight control of general pay increases produced some problems. For the first time, since the famous strike by sewing machinists at Ford which in 1969 provided such an impetus to the Equal Pay Act, important strikes occurred about equal pay. *The Times* 'Business News' in June 1973[1] reported a number of strikes called by APEX (formerly the Clerical and Administrative Workers Union) which with its large female membership is particularly concerned with the proper implementation of equal pay. This union was bringing pressure on a number of employers, notably GEC, to pay larger increases to men than women and subsequently to close the new differential between male and female jobs by one third, as permitted by government policy. APEX disputed the equal cash increases to men and women which were proposed by a number of companies. The union argued that not only would the men be held back by such a proposal but that the women would also ultimately suffer as the men's rates which they would receive in 1975 would be lower than if the men received 4 per cent + £1.00 on their rates of pay. Other issues were also involved, for example, the unilateral application by one management of job-evaluation results which they had introduced to establish the basis for equal pay. APEX contested management's right to impose job-evaluation results unilaterally and similar problems may be expected in the future as some companies attempt to minimize the effects of the Equal Pay Act. Certainly the government's pay limit created problems as far as equal pay and its implementation were concerned. It highlighted one possible effect of the Equal Pay Act on men, who are in a group for pay purposes with a large number of women. The government's pay limit established under Stage Two of the Counter-Inflation Policy in 1973, often had the effect of reducing the amount of such men's pay increase as the following example will illustrate.

Group A
    1,000 men earning on average £30 per week.
    Government 'norm' permits £1 × 1 000 = £1 000

$$\text{plus } \frac{4}{100} \times 30 \times 1000 \qquad\qquad = £1\ 200$$

$$\overline{\qquad\qquad}$$
$$£2\ 200$$
                              or *£2.20 increase*

Group B
    250 men earning on average £30 per week.
    750 women earning on average £20 per week.
    £1+4 per cent for men   = £250+£300 = £550
    £1+4 per cent for women = £750+£600 = £1 350

$$\overline{\qquad\qquad}$$
$$£1\ 900$$
                              or *£1.90 increase*

This difference of increase of 30p between the groups represents the following percentage increases:

    Group A men   = 7.3 per cent on average
    Group B men   = 6.3 per cent on average
    Group B women = 9.5 per cent on average

Where a general increase is negotiated on the basis shown for

Group B, the higher-paid male workers are particularly affected. Not only is their increase reduced by the effect of the high proportion of women in the group, but they also suffer a further reduction from what they might reasonably expect, by reason of the 'across the board' nature of the increase. Increases in this form are popular with the trade unions because they favour their lower-paid members; it is currently a major objective of many general and industrial unions to improve the relative position of the low paid and such 'across the board' increases accordingly find favour with union negotiators. However, the higher-paid worker suffers particularly where a statutory government pay limit is imposed. The effect of government pay policies including that of the Equal Pay Act, on the earnings levels and thus the attitudes of skilled male workers must be carefully considered in the future. While government policy currently highlights this trend, it is likely to continue in a free bargaining situation. Evidence for this can be formed from the public sector where equal pay has applied for non-manual groups since the late 1950s. In the teaching and nursing professions which have large numbers of women, the effect of equal pay appears to have been to reduce salary levels for men to an uncompetitive level and in the case of the teachers to foster a salary system which gave less than adequate encouragement or reward to the experience and service of the career teacher. This, at any rate, appears to be the view of the National Association of Schoolmasters which has found difficulty in reaching agreement on negotiating objectives with the National Union of Teachers (of which most women teachers arc members).

If the Equal Pay Act has a similar effect in the private sector, certain industries where female employees are in the majority such as clothing and footwear, or where they constitute a large minority group, for example, textiles and food, drink and tobacco, may be faced with industrial-relations problems. Skilled or experienced male workers will not readily allow their relative pay position to worsen and there may be conflict within and between unions about the form of pay increases. Fears of such developments may account for the relative lack of enthusiasm for equal pay which can be found within certain unions and which has been the subject of comment by, for example, the Office of Manpower Economics. Where such a situation might arise, inactivity by employers is inadvisable. The problem is most unlikely to go away and a programme of information and consultation with the unions is recommended. On the basis of a full analysis of the implications of equal pay for an industry or company, a phased programme can be prepared and negotiated which will establish a basis for containing any problems arising from hostility by male employees. If the detailed provisions of the Equal Pay Act are explained fully to such men and a carefully prepared programme to satisfy its provisions communicated to them, future industrial-relations problems with key groups of employees may be overcome. Prevarication, or a negative approach is likely to store up serious problems for the future and harden attitudes which will make their resolution more difficult.

INTERPRETATION OF THE ACT

The Equal Pay Act gives the responsibility for interpreting and enforcing its provisions to the Industrial Arbitration Board and to industrial tribunals. Under regulations made in 1972, an appeal against an industrial tribunal's decision on a point of law may be made to the National Industrial Relations Court. However, with one exception which will be mentioned later, none of these bodies will give any decisions on questions about equal pay until the Act comes into force on 29 December 1975. Until they are able to give authoritative interpretations of the Act, many questions on its application will remain speculative. The layman should be aware of the lawyers' view of this statute for after 1975 lawyers' interpretations of the Equal Pay Act will affect industry to an increasing extent. The following is a not unrepresentative statement by one of the most distinguished academic lawyers in the field of industrial relations:

> This [Equal Pay Act] is one of the statutes where accuracy is rather important and I have to say at the outset . . . that

one of the things that distresses me about this statute is the extraordinary obscurity of some of its provisions (Professor K. W. Wedderburn, at BIM conference on equal pay at Hilton Hotel, London, 14 October 1970).

The obscurities to which Professor Wedderburn refers are particularly to be found in the following sections of the Act:

1 The definition of like work, that is work of a broadly similar nature (section 1). The only explanation that can assist in clarifying this crucial clause is that 'regard shall be had to the frequency or otherwise with which any such differences [between a woman's work and the work of men] occur in practice as well as to the nature and extent of the differences'. The legal profession is likely to find this highly ambivalent definition will give them a field day as difficulties of interpretation become widespread after 1975.

2 The definition of 'establishment' and of 'associated employer' (sections 1(2) and 1(6)(c)). The Act does not give any guidance on what the word establishment really means. Similarly, two companies are to be judged as associated employers if one is a company of which the other directly or indirectly has control. However, there is no definition in the Act of what 'control' means.

3 The definition of 'equal treatment' (sections 1(1), 1(4) and 1(5)). It would appear that the Act makes it a legal requirement to provide equal treatment in regard to contractually binding terms and conditions of employment. If this is the case, there is a potential area of dispute about all forms of discretionary payments, for example, sick pay schemes, discretionary bonuses and so on.

These then would appear to be perhaps the most important aspects of the Act which are obscure and which only case law will clarify. The burden of interpretation will fall on the industrial tribunals—those 'dustbins of the Parliamentary draftsmen who deal with British industrial legislation' as Professor Wedderburn has described them. Whenever there has been a problem of definition in employment or industrial-relations legislation, whether under the Industrial Training Act, Redundancy Payments Act, Industrial Relations Act or the Equal Pay Act, it seems to be given to the industrial tribunals to sort out. The number of tribunals has increased with the demands made on them and they now cope with the numerous cases about redundancy and unfair dismissal arising from the Redundancy Payments and Industrial Relations Acts. This load will increase again when the Equal Pay Act comes into force and there is quite likely to be a large number of cases in the first few years after 1975. Many of these cases will be complicated and will occupy more of the time of the tribunals proportionately than those with which they deal now. It may be expected therefore that more lawyers will be involved in equal pay cases than in the redundancy and dismissal cases.

Any woman who believes that she is not receiving equal treatment to men may refer her claim for such treatment to an industrial tribunal. Such a reference may be made within six months of the date of termination of employment as well as during employment. Significantly, a woman may claim arrears of remuneration up to a maximum period of two years prior to the submission of her claim to the tribunal. Employers should take particular notice of this retrospective aspect of the Equal Pay Act. A test case brought by a woman employee on behalf of a larger group could prove to be very expensive for an employer if she succeeds. Not only will the employer in such a case have to pay the increase perhaps retrospectively for a long period of time to other women who do the same job as the successful appellant, but the effect on other women's differentials may be of great significance.

Imagine a company employing a large number of women manual workers on a light-electrical assembly process. The women are paid on a number of rates relating to the complexity and skill requirements of their work. In the assembly shop are a number of male jobs and, two years after the Equal Pay Act comes into force, a woman assembly worker successfully claims to an industrial tribunal that she should receive equal treatment to one of these male jobs. In such a situation not only will the woman receive retrospective payment, perhaps for the full two-year period, but the company will find it most difficult to avoid paying increases to all other women in the assembly shop to maintain existing differentials. The effect on labour costs and on industrial relations could be serious, particularly if a back-payment has to be made to all the women. It is quite likely that such cases will occur in the years immediately after the Equal Pay Act comes into force and this prospect should be a major incentive to employers to plan their policy on the effects of the Equal Pay Act carefully and well in advance of the last week of 1975. However, it is not only the industrial tribunals which will be concerned with enforcement and interpretation of the Equal Pay Act.

THE INDUSTRIAL ARBITRATION BOARD

Section 3(4) of the Equal Pay Act sets out certain responsibilities given to the Industrial Court in relation to the application and interpretation of the Act. These references to the Industrial Court are likely to be confusing as the Industrial Court has been renamed the Industrial Arbitration Board. Therefore where the statute refers to the Industrial Court, it is now the Industrial Arbitration Board which has these responsibilities.

These responsibilities are of considerable importance. The Department of Employment 'shot in the arm' publication *Equal Pay—What are you Doing about it?* puts it succinctly. 'The Industrial Arbitration Board (IAB) and the industrial tribunals will be responsible for interpreting the Equal Pay Act. But the IAB will not be able to give advisory rulings until the beginning of 1975 . . . ' (Page 9.)

The first point to note is that the IAB is given a specific role before the Act comes into force. Collective agreements and employers' pay structures may be referred to the Board at any time during 1975. In this final year of the transitional period, the Board can be asked to give advice about any changes which should be made to such agreements and pay structures to ensure that they are not discriminatory under the terms of the Act. Either party to a collective agreement may make such a reference to the Board, while an employer may make a similar request for advice on his company's pay structure. Unlike the situation after the transitional period has ended (29 December 1975) the Secretary of State cannot make such references on his own initiative during 1975.

So, during 1975, the Board has an advisory role and can give guidance and help where serious problems on the effect of the Equal Pay Act exist and where the party or parties involved seek the Board's help.

After the end of 1975, the role and responsibilities of the Board are extended and may be of great significance. The most important aspect of the Board's powers relate to collective agreements. Any such agreement from 1976 onwards which contains any provision 'applying specifically to men only or to women only' (section 3(1), Equal Pay Act) may be referred to the Board for amendment with a view to removing such discriminatory references. Section 3(4) of the Act lays down in quite specific terms how such an amendment must be made by the Board.

The Board must extend to both men and women any provision in an agreement which is limited to either men only or women only. Where, for example, there are two rates of pay in an agreement, one for men and the other for women for the same type or level of work, then the Board must eliminate the lower of the two rates. This principle would also apply where an agreement lists a number of rates of pay for men by category of work but only one rate for women. In such a case the Board would be required to raise the women's rate to the lowest rate in the agreement. Similarly the Board must amend any other terms and conditions in a collective agreement which discriminates on the basis of sex.

References on such matters to the Board can be made by either party to the agreement or by the Secretary of State for Employment, with or without the consent of the parties concerned. The Board has similar powers in relation to employers' pay structures and to wage regulation orders and agricultural wages orders.

The importance of these powers of the Industrial Arbitration Board to amend collective agreements has been considered fully in Chapter 7. It is worth however re-emphasizing this importance at the conclusion of this book, for it is this aspect of the Equal Pay Act which has, or will have, the widest effect on women's levels of pay. As the report of the Office of Manpower Economics showed, over 3,500,000 women are covered by collective agreements and wages council orders.[2] All will be affected by these provisions of the Act if male rates of pay exist as a basis of comparison. So, if there is any one aspect of the Act which should be singled out for the attention of management it is this one. Companies would be well advised, therefore, to examine and analyse the effect on their women employees of any collective agreement or wages council order which applies to them, by comparing the lowest male rate of pay with the earnings of women in the company's employ. If a company is not covered by any such agreement or order but other firms in the area are covered, management should study these for this will indicate what will become the rates of pay in the local labour market. And, perhaps it is worth bearing in mind that a firm objective of the TUC is a £20.00 per week *minimum* basic rate, while the *average* earnings of all women in manufacturing industry in April 1972 were only £17.20 per week. This simple comparison may highlight the fact that for many industries and companies there is much that needs to be done to meet the requirements of the Equal Pay Act and time is running short.

REFERENCES

1. *The Times,* 10 June 1973.
2. OME Report, page 17, paragraph 47.

Appendix

Joint plan for implementation of equal pay on an industry-wide basis

NATIONAL JOINT NEGOTIATING COMMITTEE FOR THE TOBACCO INDUSTRY—A WAY TO EQUAL PAY

Management and trade unions in the industry have agreed a plan for their approach to the question of equal pay for factory employees.

Agreement was reached on this plan by the NJNC Executive Committee after detailed talks by a joint working party of management and trade union representatives of the National Joint Negotiating Committee which represents employers and employees throughout the industry.

Fully accepting the spirit of the Equal Pay Act, which requires, by law, that equal pay is introduced by December 1975, the working party dealt with four main areas:

1   Comparison of men's jobs and women's jobs.

2 The rate at which equal pay should be implemented.
3 The age at which the full rate should be paid.
4 Equal opportunities.

Comparing men's and women's jobs will help towards the principle of equal pay for equal work.

All job-evaluation schemes are to be reviewed to make sure there is no discrimination simply because of the sex of the employee.

While these reviews are taking place, if there is an increase in wages, men and women will receive equal amounts of cash across the board or in corresponding job grades.

Because of the big changes in the traditional differences between men's and women's pay and the effect these changes could have in factories, the working party felt that equal pay should not be fully implemented much before 1975. As well, they thought that to do too much too soon would be costly and would be bound to limit the amount of money available in other ways to both men and women.

But the working party thought that moves should be made towards equal pay before the law requires and that it should be phased in smoothly in the years leading up to 1975.

So they agreed to the following timetable:

During 1971: Cash increases, if any, to be paid equally to men and women either across the board, or to corresponding job grades: review of job-evaluation schemes to determine equivalent male and female jobs.

During 1972: Removal of one-quarter of the differentials between equivalent male and female rates of pay.

During 1973: Removal of one-third of the then remaining differentials.

During 1974: Removal of one-half of the then remaining differentials.

During 1975: Complete removal of differentials to achieve full equal pay.

The Equal Pay Act requires that men and women are paid the full rate at the same age and this condition could be met by fixing this common age at 21, but the working party thought this question should be looked into.

In this industry many girls have been receiving their full rate at 18, but the working party felt that to pay the new (and much higher) equal-pay rate that early would create far too much disturbance to traditional relationships, particularly since the girls will be getting substantial increases through the higher common rate anyway.

Again, they argued, because of the large number of girls employed in the industry, the additional cost would be considerable and would be bound to reduce the amount of money available for general increases and this would be unfair to the men.

But they decided to do more than the law requires and to alter the age for the full rate to 20 for women in 1973 and for men in 1974—although they realized that after 1975 this age might be renegotiated.

They also agreed a transitional stage of 19 for women in 1972 so that anyone who is once paid the full rate does not get paid less than her older colleagues while the plan is being brought in.

So, for example, if the difference between the full rates for men and women in jobs which are established as being of equal value is now £5.00 per week, all women who are now aged 18 or over would get increases of £1.25 per week in 1972, in 1973, in 1974 and in 1975, as well as any general increases paid to both men and women during the period.

If a 17-year-old girl is now getting £1.50 per week less than the full female rate she would get increases of about £1.75 per week in 1972, in 1973 and in 1974, and about £1.25 per week in 1975, as well as any general increases. (The exact size of the increases will depend on the form of the age scales now operating.)

A 16-year-old girl now on £3.00 per week less than the full female rate would get about another £1.75 per week in 1972 and in 1973, and about £2.25 per week in 1974 and in 1975, again on top of any general increases.

Of course, some young men will also benefit from the full rate being paid at 20.

The Act does not legally require it, but the working party agreed it was in the spirit of the agreement that the removal of discrimination in job opportunities should be encouraged.

But they did not think it sensible to say exactly what should be done about this until they see how people's ideas change when men's and women's pay becomes closer. Instead, a definite meeting is planned for 1973 when this will be discussed again.

These are the main points of the equal-pay plan and the reasons why a planned progression has been agreed, with opportunities for reviewing it.

The aim is a clear, rational approach to equal pay and provision has been made for the joint working party to hold further meetings next year and in following years to review the way things are going.

Bibliography

Office of Manpower Economics, *Equal Pay—1st Report on the Implementation of the Equal Pay Act 1970*, HMSO, 1972.

Industrial Society, *Implementation of the Equal Pay Act 1970* (Report number 174), Industrial Society, 1972.

G. J. Mepham, *Problems of Equal Pay*, Institute of Personnel Management, 1969.

D. T. B. North and G. L. Buckingham, *Productivity Agreements and Wage Structures*, Gower Press, 1969.

National Board for Prices and Incomes, *Job Evaluation* (Report number 83, Cmnd 3772), HMSO, 1968.

Department of Employment, *Equal Pay—A Guide to the Equal Pay Act 1970*, Department of Employment, 1970.

Department of Employment, *Equal Pay—What are you Doing about it?* Department of Employment, 1973.

Nancy Seear, 'The position of women in industry', in *Two Studies in Industrial Relations* (Research Paper number 11, Royal Commission on Trade Unions and Employers' Associations), HMSO, 1968.

Index